Seven Years Seven Ways

Surviving Your Teen and Preteen Years

Chad E. Bladow

Starrider Books
St. Louis

Starrider Books
P.O. Box 1237
Maryland Heights, MO 63043-1237

ISBN: 978-0-9791634-0-1
Library of Congress Control Number: 2007905126

Note: This book is not a substitute for professional medical care and counseling. The author's opinions and ideas are intended to be helpful and informative. This book is sold with the understanding that the author and publisher are not engaged in providing professional services in the book. If the reader requires additional assistance, help or counseling, a competent and licensed mental health professional should be consulted.

The author and publisher disclaim any responsibility for any liability, loss or risk, personal or otherwise, which is incurred as a consequence, directly or indirectly, of the use and application of the contents of this book.

Copy Editor: Chrysa Cullather
Cover Design: Vanessa Perez
Interior Design: 1106 Design

Printed in the United States of America

To my wife and my children, for believing in me.

Table of Contents

Acknowledgments vii
Charitable Contributions ix
Introduction 1

Part 1: Seven Years

1. First Fight. 9
2. Bullies and Picking Teams 19
3. Vince, The Locker Room Bully 29
4. The Trigger 37
5. The Roller-Coaster Ride. 49
6. Peering Down into the Abyss 63
7. Coming into the Light 77

Part 2: Seven Ways

8. Seven Ways to Survive and Thrive 89
9. Why Forgiveness and Understanding? 95
10. Forgiveness and Understanding: Your Peers 99
11. Forgiveness and Understanding: Your Parents
    and Yourself. 109
12. Perspective 119
13. Faith. 131
14. Gifts and Talents 143
15. Involvement 149
16. Hopes and Dreams. 165
17. Where Do I Go from Here? 177
Positive Quotations. 181
Resources 187

List of Sidebars

Chapter 1
Bullying. 14

Chapter 2
Bullying Goes High-Tech 21
If You Are Being Bullied 24

Chapter 3
Sexual Harassment 32

Chapter 4
Dating and Rejection. 42
Dealing with Anger and Emotional Pain. 44

Chapter 5
Depression. 51

Chapter 6
Surviving Grief 65
Helping a Friend—Intervention. 68
Suicidal Behavior. 72

Chapter 10
Rejection. 103

Chapter 11
Communicating with Your Parents 113

Chapter 12
Perspective Is Power—Five Paths to Perspective 120
Group Exercise—Name-Calling 122
The Teenage Brain. 125

Chapter 13
Religion and Teenagers 133
Guideposts for Your Faith Journey 134

Acknowledgments

I would like to thank my editor, Chrysa Cullather, for her amazing attention to detail. This book is truly better due to her efforts. I would also like to thank Vanessa Perez for her wonderful cover design, and everyone at 1106 Design for helping make the interior look great.

Many thanks also go to those people who gave me encouragement along the way while writing this book: Linda, Marcia, Kim, Elizabeth, Rachel, Jason, Sarah, Maggie, Vicki and Adam. Most of all I would like to thank my wife Heidi, for her continual support, trust and faith, without which this book would never have been written.

Charitable Contributions

Starrider Books will donate a portion of the proceeds from the sale of this book to two charities that help teens and preteens:

+ KUTO, Kids Under Twenty One – A St. Louis, Missouri charity that trains teens as crisis counselors who then staff a hotline to help other teens and pre-teens in crisis situations. You can learn more about KUTO at *http://www.kuto.org.*

+ Rupert's Kids – An Indianapolis, Indiana charity that helps at-risk youth learn the job skills, confidence and self-worth they need to be successful in their communities. You can learn more about Rupert's Kids at *http://www.rupertskids.org.*

Introduction

The seven years from age eleven to eighteen were the most difficult and troubling years of my life. I struggled with verbal and physical abuse from bullies, cruel rejections, low self-esteem and what would probably have been diagnosed as mild depression.

What makes my story important? It's the same story played out every year by thousands, if not millions, of otherwise normal teens and preteens who struggle with the same issues I did. For some, the struggle for self-esteem and acceptance becomes a battle between life and death.

Two of my high school classmates did not survive their own personal struggles. The tragedy of their suicides haunts me more now as an adult than it did when I was a teen. Now I know how truly precious life is; now I know how different and wonderful life can be as an adult; now I know what they have missed all these years.

The goal of this book is to help you through your teen and preteen years—to smooth out the bumps of what can sometimes feel like a wild roller-coaster ride. I want you to know you are not alone, that you can persevere, and that your true and best life is waiting for you in adulthood. I hope I can teach you all those things by telling you my story in vivid detail and explaining the strategies I used to get through the seven toughest years of my life.

Part 1 of this book tells my story from the perspective I had as a teenager. I share my joys and sorrows, my triumphs, and my anguish. Part 1 is full of real people, real conversations, and real experiences. Although the people are real, I have changed the names of every person I mention to respect their privacy. I hold no grudge against them now.

You might say my story in Part 1 isn't a sensational one. My parents didn't abuse me; I never used illegal drugs; my family wasn't wealthy, but we weren't impoverished either. I didn't always get along with my parents during the teenage years, but my home life was tolerable. But outside of that environment, I faced abuse from bullies, cruel and insensitive treatment by my peers, dangerously low self-esteem, and what were sometimes overwhelming feelings of worthlessness.

It is important to tell my story in Part 1 for three reasons. First, if you are an adolescent, you need to know you are not alone. Others have gone through the same trials that you may be going through now. Hopefully, you will see yourself, your friends, or your acquaintances through my own story and learn something about yourself and them as a result. Second, Part 1 benefits the parent or friend of a teen or preteen who may not have experienced the same difficulties during those years of life. Part 1 may help you see and feel what it is like to be in the midst of these struggles and may help you relate to your child or friend who is not having as easy of a time as you may have had. Part 1 of this book may help you see life through their eyes and understand that bullying and depression are not "rites of passage" for the teenage years; they are serious issues that need to be addressed. Finally, only by sharing those years with you can I explain in Part 2 how I survived them and, in doing so, help you to survive as well. Part 1 provides the context within which to explain the survival and coping strategies described in Part 2.

Part 2 of this book is devoted to sharing with you the seven ways I coped with the challenges of my teen and preteen years. Some of these were foundations that supported me (faith, family, involvement, and talents); others were strategies to guide me (understanding, hopes, and dreams). Not everyone has foundations like I had in my life, and even with foundations it was a struggle to survive. That's why I wrote this book—to help you recognize the foundations and strategies you already have and discover or create those you still need. I believe the seven ways presented in Part 2 will be a tremendous help during your adolescent years. They worked for me. They can work for you, too.

In Chapter 13, I discuss the ways my religious faith helped me during those seven years. You might ask, why include a chapter on religious faith when the rest of the book is not religious? The answer is simple: My religious faith was one of the strongest foundations that supported me during those years; omitting that chapter would leave a gaping hole in my story. My faith guided and supported me through dark, shadowy valleys of my life. If you have a religious faith, I believe it can support and guide you, too. If you don't have a religious faith, you can choose whether or not to read Chapter 13, but I encourage you to read it so you can get the complete story of my seven adolescent years.

Each chapter provides a group of questions titled "Your Thoughts." Your Thoughts is designed to help you think about your own life and experiences during your teen and preteen years. Be sure to take time to think of answers to these questions. You can use the Notes pages at the end of this book to write down your thoughts or use separate sheets of paper. Thinking about your life by considering these questions will help you to apply the seven survival strategies found in Part 2.

At the end of each chapter, you will find questions for group discussion. These questions are designed to stimulate a lively group discussion about the social issues related to this book. Even if you are not reading this book with a group, I recommend reading and thinking about these questions. They may lead to understanding, and understanding is the seed of healing.

Many chapters in Part 1 contain sidebars (additional informa-tion set off in a box) that contain useful information from other sources. Each of these sidebars includes a website address where you can find more information on the sidebar topic. The List of Sidebars that follows the Table of Contents can help you to quickly locate a sidebar of interest.

The Positive Quotations and Resources sections at the end of this book provide additional useful information to help you during your teen and preteen years. The Resources section is a sampling of the huge number of resources available to you—everything from books to websites to crisis hotline numbers. The books mentioned in Resources aren't just for crisis situations; many are inspirational and motivational books for any teen or preteen.

Positive Quotations contains inspirational and thought-provoking quotations that I found while looking for quotations to place at the beginning of each chapter of this book. These quotes are wonderful gems that can give you hope and faith when you need it most. Turn to Positive Quotations—or another source of uplifting quotes—whenever you need an emotional boost.

As you read this book, you will notice that I was aware of some of the seven survival strategies during my teen years, but others I can see only now, looking back from adulthood. The years have provided some distance, some separation from my emotions of the time, and more perspective to enable me to reflect more objectively. When I was in the middle of those trying years, it was difficult to have that perspective. I hope my perspective as an adult will help you to put your seven years in perspective as well.

This book is not a substitute for professional help. I am not a psychologist. I am not trained in counseling. All I can offer is my story, my survival strategies, and myself as an example of someone who survived the teen and preteen years. If the coping strategies in this book don't help you, invent your own or find other self-help books. Don't be afraid to seek professional counseling. Talking directly to someone about your problems can provide a type of healing that cannot be achieved by reading a book.

Having said that, I do believe the seven ways described in this book can help everyone, even adults who may be struggling with issues particular to adults. The seven ways are "tried and true." I know, because I used them successfully whether I realized it at the time or not. Surviving those years made it possible for me to find the gift of my real life—my best life—in adulthood.

Can I promise you that your life will change as dramatically and positively as mine did after high school? No, I can't. I don't know what the future holds for you any more than I know what it holds for myself. One thing is certain: You have to survive your teen and preteen years to discover the gifts and joys that your life has waiting for you in adulthood. It is my hope that this book will help you to do that.

Part 1: Seven Years

1

First Fight

If we could read the secret history of our enemies, we should find in each man's life sorrow and suffering enough to disarm all hostility.

—HENRY WADSWORTH LONGFELLOW

"Hey, Bladow!" a voice called from behind me. I twisted in my desk chair, looking over my left shoulder to see who was talking to me. It was a classmate who I'll call Jed. He was a tall, lanky, blond-haired boy who sat in the row to my left and a few seats behind in my sixth-grade English class.

He stared me in the eye and said, "After class we're gonna fight. You and me."

I turned back to face the front of the room without responding to him, hoping that if I ignored him, he might drop his challenge. Class hadn't started yet; students were still entering the room, taking their seats. I wished with all my heart that the teacher would start class immediately so I could avoid dealing with Jed.

"Hey, Bladow, I'm talking to you!" he continued emphatically, this time quietly so he wouldn't draw the attention of the teacher. I turned to look at him again.

"Did you hear me?" he said. "After class we're gonna fight."

"No," I said. "I'm not going to fight you. It's not going to prove anything." I quickly faced the front of the classroom again.

I was shaking. I wasn't sure if my usual "ignore-the-bully-and-he-will-go-away" technique would work this time. I had never fought Jed before, nor anyone else for that matter. There was no way I could have provoked him by anything I had said because I had never spoken with him before. I knew him only by name.

Unfortunately, I had grown familiar with verbal taunts and teasing over the years before sixth grade. I was accustomed to being called names like Fatso, Fatty Chaddy, and "metal mouth" (referring to my braces), but it had never escalated to fighting. I wasn't overweight anymore by sixth grade, but it didn't matter. I was a shy, weak, klutzy, brainy "goody-two-shoes" who never got into trouble and who had to wear corrective dress shoes to correct my splayed feet to school instead of tennis shoes like everyone else. What more could a bully ask for? I was the perfect target.

Finally, after seconds that seemed like hours, class started. Maybe he would just drop it, I hoped. I decided to sneak out quickly at the end of class to avoid him. I wasn't stupid. He was at least six inches taller than I was with arms easily six inches longer than mine. It wouldn't even be a contest; it would be more like a beating, with me as the punching bag.

At the end of English, I slipped out quietly and walked quickly to science class down a side hallway. My sense of relief was palpable—my racing heart slowed and my body relaxed. I had escaped.

But my escape was only temporary. The beginning of English class the next day was a repeat of the day before.

"Hey, Bladow!" Jed began again before class started.

I slowly, reluctantly, shifted in my seat to face him.

"Today we're gonna fight. Just you and me. Got it?" he said with a quiet, menacing tone, still trying to keep the teacher from overhearing.

"I'm not going to fight you, Jed," I replied and turned to face the front of the room. Class started. Again I thought I had bought some time. I decided to use the same strategy to avoid fighting—sneak out at the end of class. It had worked once before; it could work again. I was frightened, though. I could feel fear turning my muscles to jelly.

At the end of class, I left quickly, but as I passed the next classroom and headed down the hall to science class, I felt a stabbing punch hit me square in the back between the shoulder blades. There was nothing left to do, no way to escape, so I threw down my books and wheeled around in anger to face him.

Before I had even finished turning around, he punched me again, right in the mouth. It was a stinging, eye-watering punch. I started to lift my fist, but he recoiled and punched me in the mouth again. I swung my right fist at him, but his arms were so much longer than mine that I couldn't reach him, yet he could reach me. He kept pounding me in the face as fast as he could bring his arm back and punch again.

After what must have been a dozen punches to the mouth, with me trying in vain to hit him back, I lowered my head and lunged forward, grabbing his gray and white plaid shirt to try to pull him over or throw him off balance. Rip! His shirt tore nearly in half, but he was still standing.

"That's enough! Knock it off!" Finally, a teacher had arrived to put a stop to it. I don't remember which teacher it was—just that he was a man. I was vaguely aware, only then, that a crowd of students had gathered to watch the fight.

I glanced at Jed. He was cradling his punching hand in his other hand. His knuckles were bloody, but I couldn't tell whether it was blood from my mouth or from cuts on his knuckles. Blood dripped, almost ran, out of my mouth. He had repeatedly punched me directly over my sharp, metal braces, cutting the inside of my upper lip, which hurt as if it had been stung by a bee.

"Off to the principal's office! Both of you!" the teacher yelled.

"Good!" I replied angrily. I wanted justice, and I wanted it right then and there.

As Jed, the teacher, and I headed to the principal's office, I took the lead. I was furious, absolutely livid. I had done nothing wrong. I had done nothing to start a fight. I had done the right thing—tried to walk away and avoid a confrontation.

Calvin and Hobbes ©1987 Watterson. Dist. By Universal Press Syndicate. Reprinted with permission. All rights reserved.

The blood dripped out of my mouth fast enough that I had to cup my hand in front of my chin to keep it from getting all over my shirt. As we neared the principal's office, I stopped at a drinking fountain to rinse some of the blood from my mouth. Thankfully, I couldn't feel any loose teeth. Maybe the braces had held everything in place.

In my thoughts, I dared the teacher to scold me for stopping at the drinking fountain, delaying our trip to the principal's office. I wanted to give him a piece of my mind, wanted to lash out at someone, but he didn't say a word. He just waited for me to finish.

We were escorted to the vice principal's office because the principal wasn't in at the time. The vice principal, who I'll call Mr. Jones, was briefed by the teacher who broke up the fight, then he showed us into his office.

"Have a seat, gentlemen," he began, pointing to two chairs in front of his desk. It was a small office, barely big enough for his desk, two chairs, and a few filing cabinets. Floor-to-ceiling dark brown paneling covered the walls. He had a matching dark brown, Formica-topped desk. Even the carpet was dark.

My mind raced. Where was the principal? He knew me. He knew my family. He knew my mom, a teacher in the same school district but at a different school. The principal, who I'll call Mr. Keller, would know in a second what really happened. Mr. Jones, however, was a stranger to me, having just started working at our school that year. I didn't know what to expect from him.

"Well . . ." he began, then paused for effect. "Maybe I should suspend you both for fighting."

Now I was even more furious. I wanted justice, and I had expected an authority figure like Mr. Jones to be fair. Instead, I was receiving the third degree for being the victim. He didn't know what happened, didn't care to hear the facts, and didn't want to make an effort to be fair. All he wanted was to dole out punishment or make us afraid of him. It made me feel doubly wronged, by both Jed and him.

He silently stared at each of us in turn, then said, "Or maybe I should call your parents."

"Good!" I said firmly and with a hint of anger. "Let's call them right now. I want them to know what happened."

A weak, whining voice to my left said, "No, please don't. Don't call my parents. Please don't." It was Jed. I looked at him, and, to my disbelief, he started crying. Mr. Tough Guy who absolutely *had* to fight me, who insisted on beating me up, was crying. I was disgusted and revolted. This bully was a cowardly sheep in wolf's clothing.

As I watched him cry, I wondered why he was crying. Did his parents beat him if he got into trouble? Was he worried about what would happen to him at home if his parents found out? I had no way of knowing, and I didn't want to ask, but the question softened me a little. I began to feel some pity for him mixed with the loathing I still felt.

The door to Mr. Jones' office opened. Mr. Keller walked in and squeezed past Jed's chair so he could face us from the other side of the desk. Inwardly I breathed a big sigh of relief.

"I'm surprised you didn't defend yourself more, Chad," he offered. Apparently, some of the onlookers had filled him in on the play-by-play action of the fight. I appreciated his unspoken acknowledgment that I was not at fault, but I was also annoyed. How did he expect me to defend myself against someone much taller and stronger than myself, someone who was more practiced at fighting than I was? Still, I felt relieved he was there. Now I had an advocate on my side, someone who would implicitly believe my side of the story.

The questioning ended shortly after that because there wasn't much more to say about the incident. After Jed received an ice pack for his knuckles, and I one for my rapidly swelling upper lip, we were sent to our next class.

Bullying

What is bullying?
- ✦ Repeated attempts to harm someone who is weaker, "different" or more vulnerable.
- ✦ Direct attacks such as hitting, threatening or intimidating, hurtful teasing and taunting, name calling, sexual harassment or comments, and stealing or damaging belongings.
- ✦ Indirect attacks such as spreading rumors or gossip, attempting to damage someone's reputation, or encouraging others to reject or exclude someone.

How common is bullying?
- ✦ Nearly thirty percent of teens in the United States (or more than 5.7 million) are estimated to be involved in bullying either as the aggressor, as a target of bullying, or both.
- ✦ In a national survey of students in grades six to ten, thirteen percent reported bullying others, eleven percent reported being the target of bullies, and another six percent said they bullied others and were bullied themselves.
- ✦ A 2002 study by the Family and Work Institute reported that one third of youth are bullied at least once a month.

For more information:

National Youth Violence Prevention Resource Center
http://www.safeyouth.org/scripts/teens/bullying.asp

National Crime Prevention Council
http://www.ncpc.org/topics/bullying

That night when my Dad arrived home, I was waiting for him at the front door. There was no way to disguise my huge, swollen upper lip, so I decided to face the issue head on.

As soon as he saw me, he asked emphatically, "What happened?"

At that moment, all the emotions of the day—anger, resentment, fear, frustration, embarrassment, and violation—came pouring out of me in great heaving sobs. It took a while before I could even blurt out between tears, "I . . . got . . . in . . . a . . . fight." He put his arms around me and held me until my sobbing subsided enough for me to explain in more detail. I was afraid he would be angry with me for getting in a fight, but he just hugged me and held me.

It felt so good to be a kid at that moment, to have a parent who could shoulder some of the pain I felt, to have a parent who cared and loved me when it felt like no one else did. After I calmed down, I told my dad the first and last name of the boy who started the fight. When I said his last name, my dad got a quizzical look on his face.

"I wonder . . ." he said.

"What?" I asked.

"Well, I got in a fight with someone with the same last name when I was in middle school, but his first name was Jim. It was a different school district, but Jim might be Jed's father. I guess the fruit doesn't fall far from the tree."

It was the first time I had heard that expression, and I have never known a more apt analogy. It was quite possible that Jim and Jed were father and son, or at least related. We lived in a semirural area of Wisconsin where the same last name usually implied a relation.

The next day at school, Jed and I crossed paths in the hallway.

"How's your lip?" he asked, noticing my still swollen mouth. I sensed he felt some regret for what had happened.

"It's OK," I replied. "It doesn't hurt too much. How are your knuckles?"

He grinned. "Not too bad. Just some little cuts."

We acted differently that day. It seemed we shared the strange, subtle camaraderie of two people who had both survived a mutual ordeal. He spoke to me in a kinder, more mature manner than he had the previous two days. The experience had changed us both.

Later that day, English class met in the library; Jed and I sat at the same table. I think we both felt the need for resolution.

"Hey, Jed," I said to him. "I was talking with my dad last night, and he recognized your last name. Is your dad's name Jim?"

"Yeah, it is."

I told him the name of the middle school my father had attended and asked him if his dad had gone to the same school.

"Yeah, I think he did," he said.

"I think our dads went to school together. Isn't that weird?" I asked. I told him my dad's name and asked him to check with his dad as well.

"OK, I will," he said.

I didn't bother to mention that our fathers might have been in a fight in middle school too. I figured he would find out on his own, if his father chose to tell him. The following day Jed confirmed that his father had gone to school with my father. Life is strangely ironic sometimes.

Jed never bothered me again, never even threatened to. For a few days, we exchanged "hellos" when passing in the halls, but we never spoke about the fight again. After those first few days, we never spoke with each other again; we had resumed being strangers.

My dad's caring response and the irony of the situation helped me to deal with the emotional effect of the fight, but only to a point. I still struggled with a lingering mixture of emotions: fear, resentment, and confusion. Why had Jed chosen me? Why didn't he choose someone else? Why did he single me out for no good reason? What was it about me that would make someone want to bash my teeth in? Would someone else want to beat me up? Who? When?

I wasn't sure which of my many emotions about the fight was the strongest, but one thing was certain: I didn't like how I felt.

Reflections

Whether you face bullies trying to beat you up, mean girls belittling you and calling you names, people laughing at you when you can't do even one sit-up in gym class, or people trash-talking you behind your back, it hurts. It hurts bad. If you're like me, you internalize it and begin to believe it or at least begin to think less of yourself as a result.

Some people can brush off such meanness and not let it bother them, knowing that the bullies and mean girls are the ones who have a problem, not themselves. I wasn't able to do that very well when I was young. Only now, as an adult, can I see clearly that the bullies had a problem, not me. That's true for you too: It's not you who has a problem, it's them.

Bullies bully you, call you names and trash-talk you because they're getting something out of it for themselves— the cheap thrill of being cruel and making themselves look better than someone else. But it's a brief thrill. Bullies and the mean crowd have to keep doing it over and over again to feel better about themselves or release some pent up anger and pain they are feeling about their own lives.

In Chapter 12, I talk about putting your current situation in perspective, including dealing with bullies. In Chapter 10, I discuss forgiveness—how I forgave Jed and how you can forgive the bullies or mean girls in your life.

Your Thoughts

✦ Have you ever experienced bullying? How did it make you feel? How long did that feeling last?

✦ What problems do you think the bully was experiencing in his (or her) life that caused him to behave the way he did? Do you think a friend put him up to it? Do you think he was trying to bolster his own self-esteem but chose a very poor way to do it?

✦ If you don't have a caring parent you can turn to, is there anyone else you can turn to for support? An aunt or uncle, a teacher, a neighbor, a coach?

Group Discussion

✦ Share each other's experiences with bullies. Discuss the bullies' motivations. What do you think they hoped to achieve by bullying? Do you think they were aware of the real motivations behind their actions?

✦ Is walking away from a potential fight the best way to deal with a threat from a bully? What else might work?

✦ Who is the best person to turn to for support after a bullying or abusive experience? A friend? Parents? Counselors? Clergy (e.g., pastor, priest, rabbi)? Why?

✦ My parents offered to send me to martial arts classes so I could defend myself from bullies, but I hated violence and just wanted to avoid the issue (for better or worse), so I turned down their offer. Do you think learning martial arts would have helped? Why or why not?

2

Bullies and Picking Teams

What you keep by you, you may change and mend;
but words, once spoken, can never be recalled.

—WENTWORTH ROSCOMMON

Jed was the first serious bully I encountered, but unfortunately, he was not the last. More bullies followed. They came out of the woodwork over the next few years. It was as though they were part of a bullying "hotline" where they exchanged names of potential victims. The bullying ranged from verbal teasing and name calling to physical bullying: hitting or threatening to hit. Sometimes the bully was a complete stranger, shoving me up against a locker with a loud clang, laughing as he walked away past the hall monitor teacher, who usually did nothing about it. More often, the bully was someone I knew, someone in my class or the next-higher grade. Sometimes he was even a friendly acquaintance who later turned on me.

One such acquaintance was a guy I'll call Nick. He was in eighth grade; I was in sixth. I had met him the previous fall on an ecology/ nature retreat weekend in northern Wisconsin at a camp deep in the north woods. At the time, Nick went to a neighboring school district where my dad taught eighth grade math and science. My dad had arranged to take me along on his school's annual eighth grade retreat that year, although I went to a different school district and was two years younger than the other kids on the trip.

Nick befriended me during the retreat. He thought it was both cool and funny that "coach's kid," as he referred to me, was along that weekend (my Dad was a basketball coach at his school). We joked around good-naturedly and enjoyed each other's company that weekend. I knew he wasn't the model student, but I enjoyed the time we shared and the fun we had. Hanging around with eighth graders, who seemed to me at the time to be nearly adults, made me feel mature and older. I liked that.

Later that school year, his family moved into my school district, and he started attending my middle school. The good-natured joking and friendly talk continued after his arrival.

"Hey, it's coach's kid!" he would say in passing in the hall with a grin on his face.

"Hey, it's Nick!" I would always reply with a smile.

One day, not long after he started at my school, I was walking toward him in the hall where he was standing with his new group of "cool" eighth-grade friends.

"Hey, Nick," I greeted him as usual and smiled. I remember thinking it was strange that this time he didn't smile or reply. He just looked at me without saying anything.

As I passed him, he reached behind me and, with a huge shove, sent my books, folders, and papers exploding out of my hands and flying down the hallway. They landed all over the place, my books sliding across the tiled floor.

He and his buddies laughed.

"Knock it off Nick!" I said angrily, turning back toward him.

He punched me hard in the arm, hard enough to make it really sting, then said, "Whatcha gonna make of it, huh?"

He stood there with his arm and fist cocked in a ready-to-throw-a-punch stance, hoping for a response. I knew once again it wouldn't

Bullying Goes High-Tech

Cyberbullying, also called electronic bullying or e-bullying, is the use of e-mail, chat rooms, instant messaging, text messaging, personal websites or blogs to threaten, insult, exclude, or embarrass other people. Cyberbullying can be as emotionally harmful to the victim as face-to-face bullying, and it can have a broader and longer-lasting effect because the bully's message can be distributed or viewed by many people over time.

To avoid being a target of cyberbullying, follow these guidelines when using the Internet or any electronic communication tool:

✦ Do not give out your personal information online, whether in instant message profiles, chat rooms, blogs, or personal websites.

✦ Never tell anyone your password—even your friends. People can use your password to gain access to personal information or to pretend they are you while they are bullying other people.

✦ If someone sends a mean or threatening message, don't respond. Save it or print it out and show it to your parents or a trusted adult. If the message was sent in a chat room, multiperson game site, or personal website (e.g., Facebook), follow the site host's instructions for reporting abusive or inappropriate behavior.

✦ Don't open e-mails from someone you don't know.

✦ Don't join in when you see someone being cyberbullied. Bullying online might seem harmless, but it isn't.

✦ Ask your parents to contact the police if you receive or witness cyberbullying messages that involve threats of violence, obscene or harassing phone calls or text messages, stalking, hate crimes, or child pornography.

Sources

National Crime Prevention Council
http://www.ncpc.org/teens/cyberbullying.php

U.S. Department of Health and Human Services
http://stopbullyingnow.hrsa.gov/adult/indexAdult.asp?Area=cyberbullying

be a fight, just a beating. He was two years older, bigger, tougher, and stronger. I turned away and started picking up my scattered books and papers. Nick and his friends walked away, laughing. Other people passing by in the hall kicked my books further away or purposely stepped on my papers, leaving shoe prints on them. It was just like a scene in a movie, one where the geeky kid is wearing a sign on his back that says "Hit me." I wasn't wearing a sign, though. Apparently, none was necessary.

In the back of my mind, a little voice asked again, "Why would someone do this to me? What is it about me that would make him do this? Nick seemed to like me before today." The little voice had no answers to my questions. The fact that Nick had been a friendly acquaintance and had appeared to enjoy my company made his cruel behavior all the more personal and painful.

Gym class was another place for public humiliation. I was weak and uncoordinated, a total klutz. If I didn't realize on my own how unathletic I was, there was the picking of teams to drive home the point. The gym teacher selected team captains, usually jocks, who then selected people for their teams, one at a time.

"I'll take John," one captain would call out.

"I'll take Mike," the other would say.

My self-esteem ratcheted down a notch with each name they called out. As the pool of potential teammates dwindled to three or four, I was usually still waiting to be picked.

I remember one such team selection in elementary school. The pool of unselected classmates was down to two—me and another kid who had minor, but noticeable, physical disabilities. The next team captain to pick a person said to the other captain, "Nah, I don't want either of them, you can have them both."

Unless you've experienced it, you can only imagine how terrible that makes you feel. You're not even at the bottom of the picking list; you're the leftover refuse that no one wants. You're undesirable, worthless, an unwanted handicap, a burden. No matter how many good things people say about you, you never forget a moment like that. You never forget that type of rejection.

Calvin and Hobbes ©1988 Watterson. Dist. By Universal Press Syndicate. Reprinted with permission. All rights reserved.

There was one other middle school bullying experience that, in retrospect, was actually funny, although at the time it didn't seem funny at all. Have you ever seen one of those animated cartoons that have a tough junkyard dog, like a bulldog, with a jumpy, hyperactive sidekick that follows him around, such as a Chihuahua or poodle? The Chihuahua keeps running around the bulldog, panting fast, and saying, "Ya gonna beat him up, boss? Huh? Huh? Ya gonna beat him up?" Well, this bullying incident was just like that.

The bulldog, a kid I'll call Kyle, decided he wanted to fight me. Kyle had lots of freckles and matching bright reddish-orange hair, poorly cut in the shape of an inverted bowl. His two large, top front teeth were completely capped with silver. I assumed his teeth had been cracked or broken in another fight. Kyle was a scrapper—stocky, strong, built for fighting, and apparently well practiced at it.

Instead of selecting English class to announce his intentions as Jed had, he chose the indoor recess period in the gym after lunch. For several days he had been asking, "So, Bladow, you wanna fight me?" Yeah, right, I thought to myself, about as much as I want a hole in my head.

Finally, one day, he cornered me in a side hallway off one end of the gymnasium. It was a usually deserted, short hallway leading to a little-used exit door. It was my worst fear for the location of a fight, a place without teachers supervising or other students to see what happened, a place where I would get a royal beating and be left in a crumpled heap with no one to stop it.

There was no one else in the hallway, just me, Kyle and his sidekick, Chihuahua Boy, a short, scrawny, brown-haired boy. The only other objects in the hallway were portable volleyball net posts that could be wheeled into the gym for physical education class. With nowhere else to go, I stood on the metal base of one of the posts, strategically placing the post between Kyle and myself.

"OK, Bladow, come on, let's fight," he began.

I stood as best I could on the volleyball post base, my shoes frequently slipping on its smooth, curved metal surface. When I didn't respond, he said, "C'mon, Bladow, let's fight!"

Chihuahua Boy chimed in, adding, "You're dead meat, man."

I had visions of a bloody nose and black eyes. I desperately wanted to find a way out, so I took a gamble.

"No, I'm not going to fight you," I said flatly.

"What do you mean you're not going to fight me," he said. "C'mon, let's fight."

If You Are Being Bullied

✦ **Talk to your parents or an adult you can trust, such as a teacher, school counselor, or principal.** Many teens who are targets of bullies do not talk to adults because they feel embarrassed, ashamed, or afraid, and they believe they should be able to handle the problem on their own. Other teens believe that involving adults will only make the situation worse. It might be possible to solve it on your own, but find a trusted adult who can help you develop a plan to end the bullying and provide you with the support you need. You don't have to do it alone.

✦ **Don't blame yourself for the bullying.** Bullying is more about what the bully is getting out of bullying (a thrill, feeling of power) than it is about you.

✦ **Don't let bullies know how much they upset you.** If bullies know they are getting to you, they are likely to torment you more. If at all possible, stay calm and respond evenly and firmly or else say nothing and walk away. Sometimes you can make a joke, laugh at yourself, and use humor to defuse a situation.

- ✦ **Don't retaliate.** That can make matters worse and you will likely be the person getting in trouble, not the bully.
- ✦ **Act confident. Hold your head up, stand up straight, make eye contact, and walk confidently.** A bully will be less likely to single you out if you project self-confidence.
- ✦ **Try to make friends with other students.** A bully is more likely to leave you alone if you are with your friends. This is especially true if you and your friends stick up for each other.
- ✦ **Avoid situations where bullying can happen.** If at all possible, avoid being alone with bullies. If bullying occurs on the way to or from school, you may want to take a different route, leave at a different time, or walk with other students to school or the bus stop.
- ✦ **If necessary, take steps to rebuild your self-confidence.** Finding activities you enjoy and are good at can help to restore your self-esteem. Take time to explore new interests and develop new talents and skills. Read Chapter 14, Gifts and Talents.
- ✦ **Do not resort to violence or carry a gun or other weapon.** Guns and other weapons can escalate conflicts and increase the chances you will be seriously harmed. Moreover, you may do something in a moment of fear or anger that you will regret for the rest of your life. It is illegal for a teen to carry a handgun; it can lead to criminal charges and arrest.

Source

National Youth Violence Prevention Resource Center
http://www.safeyouth.org/scripts/teens/bullying.asp

"No, I'm not going to," I said. "You can beat me up if you want, but I'm not going to fight you. It's not going to prove anything. Everyone knows you can beat me to a pulp, so what's it going to prove?"

He stared at me, stunned. He wasn't sure what to say to that. I had shattered the well-established convention for this kind of thing: The strong beat up the weak, and the weak put up a half-hearted attempt at defending themselves, if only to keep up appearances. I was turning that convention upside down.

"What, are you chicken or something?" he finally responded. "C'mon, let's get going. Let's fight, unless you're chicken." He raised his fist up and shifted to the right to get a clear line of sight past the volleyball post toward my face. I shifted to my right to place the post directly between us again. He shifted back the other way, and so did I, keeping the post between us.

"I'm not going to fight you," I told him again. "You can beat me up if you want, but I'm not going to fight you."

Then Chihuahua Boy let out a laugh and said, "I don't believe it."

"What?" snarled Kyle as he turned to look at his sidekick.

"I can't believe he's standing up to you," answered Chihuahua Boy.

"Shut up!" Kyle growled at him. Turning back to me, he said, "C'mon, Bladow, let's fight. Unless you're chicken."

"No," I said, trying my best to sound calm though I was far from it. "I'm not going to fight you."

Chihuahua Boy laughed again and shook his head in disbelief. Kyle backed away, lowering his fists, looking both confused and angry.

The "fight" broke up shortly after that. Kyle didn't know what to do. He and his sidekick walked away, leaving me alone in the hallway. I came down from the volleyball base, shaking like a leaf but relieved that I had talked my way out of a serious beating. I was proud of myself for taking the high ground and avoiding a fight, but being a weakling, unable to defend myself, and the subject of ridicule, cut deeply into that pride. Still, I was glad Kyle had an ounce of honor—he didn't want to participate in a one-sided beating. Most bullies aren't like that. They'll punch you in the back even as you're walking away.

I knew these bullies were messed up kids. I knew it wasn't entirely my fault, but it was impossible not to be affected by these experiences, especially because they happened often. I started liking myself less and less, considering myself somewhat beneath other people, both as a potential friend and as a human being in general. Why did this kind of thing keep happening? What was it about me that caused it? I was weak, shy, klutzy, and brainy and that, apparently, was why the bullies wanted to beat me up. When someone wants to hurt you just because you are who you are, you begin to wonder if there is something wrong with being who you are.

Reflections

Bullying behavior tends to peak in middle school, but it can continue into high school as it did for me. It ranges from simple name calling or insulting nicknames to physical assault.

The first thing you need to know about bullying is that you are not alone. Millions of people, both boys and girls, have been the target of a bully at least once in their lives, and many have experienced bullying over and over again as I did. Trust me when I tell you that you can survive it, get through it, and bear it—many people have. That doesn't mean it will be an easy burden to bear. It's not easy at all, but you can survive it and move past it.

The second thing you need to know is that it's not your fault (unless you have also been bullying other people). Bullying has far more to do with the bully's need for attention, acceptance, or power than it has to do with you. A bully's behavior also says a lot about society's narrow stereotypes of what defines popularity or acceptance and the roles of men and women. If you don't fit those narrow stereotypes, you are likely to be an easy target for bullies. Don't change who you are just to avoid the bullies. The stereotypes are so incredibly narrow that nearly everyone falls outside their scope, so nearly everyone is a potential target of bullying. Bullies often look for the smallest, most ridiculous thing they can find for an excuse to bully: your new haircut, your size or shape (no matter what it is), the way you talk, or anything else they feel like choosing.

Lastly, the nature of bullying may be different between girls and boys, but it is bullying just the same, whether someone calls you names, is verbally cruel and hurtful, spreads rumors about you on their website, or hits you in the face with a fist. No matter who the bully is, or why they chose you, it hurts and it's wrong.

In Chapter 12, I talk more about bullies and their motivations and how I see them from my perspective as an adult. For now, remember you are not alone and you can survive!

Your Thoughts

+ If you have been in a fight or were threatened with a fight, how did you respond? Did you talk or joke your way out or did you "take your lumps" and take a beating anyway? Would you handle it differently now?
+ Did you tell an adult about the fight or did you keep it a secret? Why?

Group Discussion

+ Was I a "chicken" for trying to talk my way out of a fight? Would my pride have been hurt more, or less, if I had agreed to fight and was beaten up by Kyle?
+ Is avoiding a fight, if possible, always the best course of action? Does fighting back reduce the likelihood of another fight in the future? Why or why not?

3

Vince, The Locker Room Bully

Three things in human life are important: The first is to be kind. The second is to be kind. And the third is to be kind.

—HENRY JAMES

One of my most dreaded classes was physical education class—not only because of the humiliation of picking teams but also because I was really awful at it. I nearly always felt like I was making a fool of myself. I could barely dribble a basketball, couldn't throw any kind of ball with much accuracy, and was out of breath before I finished one lap on the track. Gym class (as we called it) was just another very blatant reminder that I wasn't good enough.

Unfortunately, my two worst fears—bullies and gym class—were brought together in one bully who I'll call Vince. Vince was a sports jock. What he lacked in height and brains, he made up for in bravados and arrogance. He literally strutted as he walked. It was obvious he thought of himself as God's gift to the school sports program, if not the world in general. He thoroughly enjoyed taunting me, primarily in the locker room at the end of gym class when the gym teachers were out of sight.

"Hey, Bladow, I better not see you in the showers, or I'll beat the crap out of you. Ya hear?" was one of his threats. I had visions of a fight and cracking my head open on the slippery tile floor, so I avoided the showers. If I had to walk past the showers, I would do it quickly so he wouldn't see me. I took him seriously. He was the kind of person who would definitely follow up on a threat to prove his power, and I also knew I didn't stand a chance against him in a fight.

"Hey, Bladow, want to sniff my jock strap?" he would ask as he waved his athletic supporter in my face and laughed. Looking back on it now, that question was so stupid, it was funny.

Another threat was, "Hey, Bladow, you better watch your stuff! If I see your locker open, I'm gonna take all your stuff out and throw it down the hall. You'll have to run out of here naked to get it all." Then he would laugh his sadistic laugh and walk away.

Calvin and Hobbes ©1988 Watterson. Dist. By Universal Press Syndicate. Reprinted with permission. All rights reserved.

He never followed through on those threats, but I wouldn't have put it past him for a moment. When he harassed me or teased me, I used my usual technique of "ignore the bully then maybe he will go away." Usually that takes the fun away from the bully, because he wants to get a reaction out of you, but in Vince's case he didn't care. He kept it up anyway, even raising his voice when he taunted and teased me so that everyone else in the locker room would hear him doing it. Apparently, he thought it made him look cool or tough.

One day he decided to elevate the level of harassment. I was sitting on one of the wooden locker room benches, bending over to reach my half-height, bright orange, metal mesh gym locker. I was working the combination lock, about to get my street clothes out to change out of my gym uniform.

The locker room had that pungent, almost overpowering locker room smell of sweaty boys and their old sweaty gym uniforms that were long overdue for washing. There was the typical loud locker room shouting between groups of boys and locker doors clanging open and shut, both made louder by the echoes off the hard concrete floor. As I opened my locker, Vince came strutting over wearing only his underwear. He stood next to me, pushed down his underwear, and exposed himself at eye level to me as I sat on the bench.

"You want some of this, don't you Bladow?" he said. "Hey? You want some?"

He moved his genitals around in a suggestive manner. I stared forward at my locker, avoiding his gaze, trying to ignore him.

"You want this, don't you Bladow, huh? Don't you?" he taunted.

He thrust himself forward, forcing me to flinch aside to avoid having his genitals touch my face.

"You want some of this?" he continued.

"Cut it out, Vince!" someone behind me said.

Finally, he stopped, pulled up his underwear, and strutted away, laughing as he went.

I didn't bother telling the gym teacher about it. Today they would call it sexual harassment. Back then, no one cared. It was just "boys being boys." I'm certain the teacher would have told me to simply "work it out" with Vince. Yeah, right.

I didn't tell my parents, either. I'm not sure why. Maybe I was too embarrassed to mention it. Maybe I assumed they would call the principal, and I was afraid that would make matters worse, rather than better.

Vince's behavior was so despicable that it was relatively easy to brush off his comments, yet he was one of the bullies I hated the most. His harassment was personal and demeaning and, unlike the other bullies, there wasn't a trace of remorse, regret, or honor in his words or behavior after the bullying was over. He enjoyed being a bully, and he intended to keep it up as long as he could.

Although I brushed off his words to some degree, he was still one more person in a line of people who seemed to take joy in bullying me. I didn't completely lose my self-esteem in the face of his or other bullies' bullying, but the frequent and persistent nature of it was burdensome and taxing, slowly whittling away my self-esteem over time.

Sexual Harassment

What is sexual harassment?
+ Unwanted or unwelcome physical contact, such as grabbing, pinching, or touching private areas of your body.
+ Sexual comments such as name-calling, starting rumors about you, making sexual jokes at your expense, or making sexual gestures at or about you.
+ Flashing or "mooning".
+ Sexual requests or requests for a date that continue after you have repeatedly said no.
+ Unwanted phone calls, e-mails, or letters that are nasty, threatening, or make you feel uncomfortable.

How common is sexual harassment?
+ Although seven of ten students know their school has a policy against sexual harassment; eighty-one percent of students have experienced either verbal or physical sexual harassment at some time while in school.
+ Six of ten students say they have experienced physical sexual harassment at some point in their school lives, with one third experiencing it often or occasionally.

What can I do if I am being harassed?
+ If you feel comfortable and safe doing so, tell the person harassing you to stop. Be clear and direct.

✦ Get a copy of your school's sexual harassment policy. It should tell you what behaviors are considered sexual harassment and how you should report such behaviors.
✦ Report the harassment to your parent(s) and an appropriate adult at your school (as indicated in your school's policy).
✦ If the harassment doesn't stop using the steps listed here, then keep a journal documenting each incident of harassment, including what happened, the names of any witnesses, and how the harassment made you feel. Take this journal to school administrators and ask them to take action to stop the harassment.

Sources:

The National Center for Victims of Crime
Teen Tools: Sexual Harassment. 2004.

American Association of University Women
Hostile Hallways: Bullying, Teasing, and Sexual Harassment in School. 2001.
www.aauw.org/member_center/publications/HostileHallways/hostilehallways.pdf

Reflections

Cruelty is in our nature. It's as old as humanity itself. Cruelty to our peers seems to peak during the junior high and high school years, but cruelty knows no boundary of age, gender, ethnicity, or race. It is a behavior that must be consciously unlearned with the help of parents, teachers, clergy, and our peers. Unfortunately, society often does little or nothing to discourage it.

Although we all experience cruelty at some time in our lives, we can choose not to listen; we can choose to brush it off, ignore it, or at least put it in a proper and healthy perspective. That isn't always easy, of course. I tended to believe the bullies and the name callers rather than brushing them off. Unless you have a big ego, it's hard not to be affected by cruel words and actions, especially if you receive them day after day.

If you can't brush them off or ignore them, try to see bullies in a humorous light. In many ways, they are tragically comical. They do and say some of the stupidest things to get attention or to appear cool or tough. Laughing at their behavior can help take the sting out of their actions. You might not want to laugh out loud in their presence—that might encourage them rather than discourage them—but laugh to yourself about it when they aren't around.

The tragic thing about bullies is that they are learning a behavior that, although it might get them some mileage in high school, it won't get them anywhere *after* high school. They will quickly find that their bullying behavior has very negative consequences as an adult—everything from losing a job or losing a spouse to losing their freedom in jail.

Some bullies see the light, though. Eventually. Many change their ways and become productive members of society. It's too bad they won't be able to look back on their teenage years with pride and self-respect.

Bullying can take many forms, ranging from mild to mean, vague to extremely personal. If you're a girl, bullying tends to be either name-calling, nasty comments or exclusion from a group. Girls are far more likely than boys to use false rumors, gossip, and lies in an attempt to make someone look bad or ruin their reputation, all for the purpose of a cruel power trip. The "queen bees" will also use cruel remarks and an aloof, superior attitude to shun those who they don't want in their inner circle of friends.

You might hear things like this:

"You're so ugly no one would want to date you."

"Why don't you just put on some makeup so you don't look so ugly."

"Who do you think you are sitting next to me?"

"Where did you get those clothes, Goodwill?"

"You're so stupid you should just curl up and die."

"You are such a loser!"

"Go away you freak!"

Obviously it gets much worse than that. I don't want to use all the curse words and foul language that can be used by bullies in this book and I don't need to. You've heard them. You know them.

For boys, bullying is often more about the narrow stereotypes of manhood. If you don't fit the macho athlete image (like me), you'll hear sniggers and laughter from the jocks when you miss the basket in basketball by several yards. Even if you don't hear comments like these, it's easy to make your own painful and unfair comparisons between yourself and the taller, more muscular boys.

No matter whether you are a boy or girl, your size and weight are always targets for bullies. Whether you are skinny or overweight, short or overly tall, they will find a way to poke fun at you for it. These are some of the most hurtful, personal comments, but if you think about it, they are also some of the most ridiculous. After all, how many people fit the narrow definition of supermodel? Unless a bully is a supermodel, who is he or she to tease anyone about looks?

Whatever the nature of the bullying, it hurts. It stabs at the very heart of our self-esteem, our self-confidence, and our self-image. No one wants to think of himself or herself as ugly, undesirable, or weird. Bullies play on that fear.

Remember you are not alone, you can persevere, and these trials can even make you a stronger person. In Chapters 12 and 13, I talk about the effects bullying had on me. Ironically, despite the emotional pain it caused, I think I'm a stronger person today because of it. I wouldn't wish bullying on anyone, of course, but surviving bullying can strengthen our ability to withstand adversity later in life.

Your Thoughts

✦ Has a bully's behavior toward you ever gone beyond name calling or fist fighting? How did you cope with it? Did you seek the help of an adult? Why or why not? If you didn't, do you wish you had now?

Group Discussion

✦ Have you ever bullied anyone? How do you feel about it now?

✦ How do you think Vince feels about the incident today? Regretful? Guilty? Proud and arrogant? What negative emotional effects might it have on him later in life?

✦ What are the boundaries between "boys being boys," "girls being girls," bullying, and sexual harassment? What behaviors or actions define sexual harassment?

✦ Why are teens or preteens often afraid to go to an adult for help? Would seeking the help of an adult make the problem worse or better? Why or why not?

✦ In a recent study, seven of ten students say they know their school has a sexual harassment policy, yet eighty-one percent say they have experienced sexual harassment of some form or another. What do you think teachers, school counselors, school administrators and parents could do to reduce the frequency of sexual harassment?

4

The Trigger

This was the most unkindest cut of all.

—WILLIAM SHAKESPEARE (JULIUS CAESAR, ACT III. SC. 2.)

There were still a few bullies in high school, and to make matters worse, I now had a serious case of teenage acne. It was pretty bad. Even the prescription acne creams and gels I tried didn't help much. It gave the bullies another name to call me: Pizza Face.

I would describe my high school self as a brainy, shy, geeky, klutzy, pimple-faced tuba player. Not exactly class president material, but there was plenty of material for teasing and name calling.

Despite the bullies and the terrible acne, the first part of my freshman year was a lot of fun, mostly because of band class. I had auditioned for the school's Symphonic Band, composed mostly of juniors and seniors, and was accepted. I considered it an honor and a privilege to be one of a small group of freshmen to be accepted into that band. The jump from middle school music to senior-level symphonic music was both challenging and exhilarating.

Band was a serious program at our school, and it was given the time, attention, and money it needed to be a program of excellence.

We had a number of great musicians in our band, some of whom later went on to professional careers in music. Most of them were the cream of the crop of students at our school. There was quite a bit of overlap between the academic honor roll and band membership. I was in my element in band class.

Besides the thrill of the music, being in a band made up largely of juniors and seniors provided interaction and friendships with upper-classmen whose relative degree of maturity I enjoyed thoroughly. It was the only class in the school that mixed freshmen through seniors in the same class. In this environment, I made more friends than I ever had in middle school. Nearly all my friends throughout high school were band friends. The low brass players, tuba and baritone horn players in particular, forged a strong bond, a sort of "low brass club."

Early in my freshman year, I quickly found myself in a small group of band friends who hung around together before and after class and at band functions. We were all involved in marching band, football pep band, and symphonic (concert) band. After playing in the pep band at football games, we frequented the local McDonald's about four miles away. Those in the group who were old enough to drive would load up their cars with the rest of us and head out for an after-game celebration (this was before the days of teenage driving restrictions). It didn't matter if our football team won or lost, we always enjoyed our time together.

For the first time in my life, I felt like I was part of a group, part of a circle of friends who liked and respected me for who I was. Perhaps it was the stark contrast to the bullying I had experienced (and was still experiencing) that made being a member of this group so enjoy-able and rewarding. To be accepted and liked gave my self-esteem a much-needed boost. I began to like myself again.

One of the members of our circle was a sweet girl who I'll call Sheri. She was a sophomore, one year older than I was. She was already an accomplished musician. Her forte was piano, but she also played a wind instrument in the band. She always greeted me with a big smile and a sincere hello. Her infectious laughter made those around her laugh and smile too.

As fall flowed into early winter and the football pep band became basketball pep band, I became more and more smitten with her. She was cute, intelligent, talented, sweet, and, to my surprise, she really seemed to like me. It was my first big crush, and I had it bad.

It took several weeks for me to summon up the courage to ask her out on a date. I had never asked anyone out on a date before, and I was extremely nervous about it. What if she said no? Did she already have a boyfriend? What do I say? How do I ask her out?

I planned in great detail how I would ask her out, rehearsing it in my mind to help calm my nerves and hoping to avoid stuttering or stumbling over my words when the time came. None of my plans worked, however, because she was always around other people, both band friends and other girlfriends. I was too shy, nervous, and unsure of myself to ask her out in front of anyone. It was hard enough to have the courage to ask her face-to-face, much less with other people watching.

One Friday night, as our group of friends headed home after a post-basketball visit to McDonald's, I was in the same carpool of friends as she was. When we got to her house to drop her off, I decided on the spur of the moment to take the opportunity to ask her out. I waited until she got out of the car and started walking up her driveway. Not wanting the others in the car to hear me, I got out and shut the door most of the way behind me.

"Sheri?" I called toward her. She turned, standing in the bright white glare of the headlights of the car. It was a cold night. There wasn't any snow on the ground yet, but frost was forming, and I could see my breath when I spoke.

As I stood beside the car, shaking slightly, I said, "Sheri . . . um, I was wondering if maybe you'd like to go out for some pizza or something sometime, like maybe this Saturday?"

"I'm busy Saturday," she replied quickly. Was it too quickly, I wondered? I hesitated for a moment, not sure how to continue. She hadn't said no, but she didn't add anything either; she was still standing there, looking at me, saying nothing.

"OK. Well, how about Sunday, then?" I offered.

"I'm busy all weekend with my family," she said, again rather quickly, but added nothing more. Again, she just stood there staring at me.

I hesitated for a long moment. Of all the people I knew, she was definitely one of the busiest people outside of school because she played in her family's band. Between practicing and weekend gigs, I knew she *was* busy. It was entirely possible that she was busy all weekend, but the speed of her reply and the way she didn't offer any more information both concerned and confused me. Was she being honest or was this rejection? I didn't know what to make of it.

"OK, well . . . maybe we can talk about it more next week at school," I replied.

I don't remember whether she said anything after that. I got back in the car, closed the door, and then we drove off. None of the others in the car asked any questions about what had just happened. Maybe they didn't care, or maybe they understood and decided not to pry.

I remember that weekend seemed to last forever. I constantly replayed the events of Friday night, desperately trying to extract an answer from any subtle hints, trying to divine what she really felt, but no amount of thinking and recollection answered my questions.

I knew she liked me, at least as a friend. That much had been obvious from how she had acted toward me that fall. But was she lying to me to put me off? Why? Why would a friend do that? After all, she was one of my friends, a member of my close-knit group of band friends. Maybe she was really busy, but then why didn't she offer any other hint or word, positive or negative, to really answer the question "do you want to go out on a date?" Had the weekend been more than two days I probably would have given myself an ulcer worrying about it.

Finally, Monday came, and I was back at school with a huge nervous knot in my stomach. I knew I would see her and talk to her, at least in band class. I desperately needed some resolution—a more definite, understandable answer. I looked for her between classes in the hallways, hoping for a moment, however brief, to talk with her.

Between morning classes, well before band class, I saw her about a quarter length of a long hallway away from me. I was close enough to see her, but not close enough to call out to her.

As I continued walking toward her, still far off, she lifted her head up and saw me, making eye contact. My heart jumped for a moment, an involuntary misbeat of hope and expectation. But then, after seeing me, I saw the expression on her face change suddenly. It was an expression that unmistakably said, "Oh God. It's him." She quickly lowered her eyes, breaking eye contact, then darted down a side hallway between us, her head lowered, eyes hidden.

I had my answer. My stomach sank, and my heart felt like a lead weight. It was as if every ounce of joy and hope suddenly drained out of my body, like water pouring out of a hole in a dam. I felt hollow, humiliated, and embarrassed.

I forced myself to walk to my next class, but I wanted to run—run as far and as fast as I could possibly run—away from that place and those feelings until I could escape them. But there was no escape. There was nowhere to go.

That humiliating incident of lowered eyes and darting down side hallways to avoid me didn't happen just once. It happened several times that day and the next whenever she saw me in a hallway. It was like a recurring bad dream, pounding shame and embarrassment into me each time it happened. It made me feel like an unclean leper. I was so completely undesirable that apparently it was offensive even to make eye contact with me.

My self-esteem collapsed. I was devastated. All the taunts and name calling from bullies had chipped away at my self-esteem until there was very little left, and that last shred of self-respect was smashed completely now. I blamed it all on myself. Dark thoughts hammered at me, stabbing me with self-hatred and loathing.

You're a freak! No one wants you. No one would ever want you. Even a friend is sickened at the idea of going out on a date with you.

The bullies and jocks were right. You're weird. You're undesirable. You're a freak. You're never going to be normal or happy. You don't deserve it anyway. Even a friend won't go out on a date with you. No, even a friend is so disgusted with the thought of dating you that she can't even stand to see your stinking face anymore, can't stand to talk to you anymore, can't stand to be friends with you anymore.

Dating and Rejection

Dating Checklist

If you want to ask someone out on a date or you are considering someone's request for a date, use the checklist below to help guide your decision:

✦ Trust your instincts or what is sometimes called your "vibes." If a feeling inside you or the proverbial "little voice in your head" says "no," then trust that feeling.

✦ Date someone because you like him or her, not just because he or she is popular or beautiful. Dating is about liking someone as a person. You have to like the person, or the relationship won't last very long.

✦ Avoid convincing yourself to date someone. In other words, if you say things to yourself like "I'm not sure I like him, but he is *really* cute so maybe I'll say 'yes.'" or "I'd rather date him than be alone," those should be a clue that you're not choosing to date someone for the right reasons. This can lead to many problems: heartache, painful rejection, even addiction to an abusive relationship.

What if I am rejected?

If someone rejects your request for a date, remember the following:

✦ As long as you asked politely and kindly and have treated the other person with respect, then the rejection isn't your fault. Don't beat yourself up emotionally for it.

✦ Remind yourself that if it wasn't meant to be, then it wasn't meant to be. Attraction has to go both ways; it can't be one-sided.

✦ Pick yourself up and move on. Of course, this is easier said than done, but the best way to deal with rejection is to accept it and move on.

Fatso. Pizza face. Weirdo. Nerd. Wimp. Loser. Last choice for the team.

The world was telling me I was worthless, and I believed every word of it. Any ounce of self-respect I had was gone. I was so distraught, the mental anguish became physical: nausea, tightness in my chest, difficulty breathing. A feeling of worthlessness as hollow as darkness and as heavy as lead filled me. I wanted to crawl in a dark corner and hide. I laid on my bed that night, curled in a fetal position, aching terribly inside, wishing the pain would just go away, wishing that somehow God would take me in the night to free me from my personal prison of pain.

After two days worth of hallway avoidances, I never saw her in the hallways again. She had learned my classes and routes, learned how to avoid seeing me at all. She even started showing up for band class just seconds before our band director began teaching. She had always arrived early before that day to socialize with friends. Now, apparently, avoiding me was more important.

From that day through the remainder of my freshman year and the rest of high school, I struggled with the roller coaster of depression. Sometimes I would angrily scrawl my emotions on blank sheets of paper. Ruled paper was too restrictive, too orderly, to contain the emotions that exploded out of my pen. Sometimes the writing would help me feel better. It was like pouring out pain, a release valve to vent some of my pent-up emotions. At other times, my writing viciously fed my inner self-loathing. I called myself all sorts of terrible things, wrote them down, and believed them all.

The following pages contain excerpts of my journaling from those years. Some of my writings wound up in the trash as soon as I wrote them. I was either too embarrassed to keep them or the angry crumpling and throwing of paper helped me to release more anger than the writing did anyway. The writings that I kept have been buried away in a filing cabinet folder until now. They are not included here because the quality of my writing was great, but because they are a window into my emotions of those years.

Dealing with Anger and Emotional Pain

Feelings of anger and emotional pain can sometimes be intense and overwhelming during our teenage years. How can you deal with them? How can you release, vent, or soften those feelings to bring them (and yourself) under control? There are a variety of tried and true techniques you can use to do just that:

✦ **Journaling.** Buy a journal from your local bookstore or make one yourself with sheets of paper stapled together. Write your thoughts and feelings in your journal anytime they feel intense and overwhelming (and also when you're feeling positive). Pour out your emotions on the paper. Don't hold back. Let it all out. When you're finished, take a deep breath and relax. You'll find your emotional load is lighter and more under control.

✦ **Exercise.** Burn off your intense feelings and anger with a brisk walk, run, bike ride, or any sport that quickly burns up energy (but check with your doctor first if you have any health conditions). Exercise hard enough to work up a sweat and feel tired afterward but not so intensely that you injure yourself, because an injury will increase your stress and anger rather than reduce it. After vigorous exercise, you'll find yourself feeling better, less angry, and more in control.

✦ **Relaxation.** Use calming and relaxing music, soft lights, and relaxing thoughts to calm your mind. Think of a favorite time in your life or your favorite place (e.g., river, mountain, lake). Imagine being there while listening to your music. Close your eyes; mentally transport yourself to another time or place. When you finish your relaxation time, you'll find your problems don't seem so overwhelming, and you might even have some new ideas of how to solve them.

✦ **Talking.** Talk about your feelings with a close friend, parent, or counselor. Choose someone who you know will be a good listener, because the goal is to release your anger or pain and get it out of your system. Be careful when using this technique with a friend because he (or she) may be dealing with his own problems and might be overwhelmed by the additional weight of your problems. Be sure to end the discussion on a calm note and thank your friend for listening.

How can I find someone to love me for who I am when I cannot stand who I am, when I don't even like who I am? I am becoming something that no one can love. I am despicable.

I find that I cannot change what I have become, what I am. I cannot imagine living my whole life as this person. It would be terrible for all those around me and a nightmare from which there is no awakening.

There is nothing precious to me anymore, except my friendships, the few that I have, and the beauty of nature. Am I to become merely a machine, a mechanism? I am no longer me.

I'm not sure who I am or was, but I know that what I am is not right.

All of the billions of years for which the stuff of stars became consciousness is wasted on the part of that grandness that is me. I am nothing, I am dust in the wind. I contain all that is, but I am nothing at all.

Oh, my God what has happened to me? What have you done to me, or rather, why must I have so much pain and unhappiness? My God, what am I to do? I need someone, I need love! I am so lonely and so desperate.

What can I do now? Just whither away and die? I hate myself so badly. I am worthless!

Is there no hope?

I am tired and sick. I don't know of anyone who can help me. Everyone has their own problems. What should I do? I know that I cannot go on as I am now.

I have such a feeble will and mind. I have no strength with which to overcome the adversity that lies within me.

*I cannot choose death. One good thing (I guess)
of my mind is that it is blank. Nothing affects me
enough anymore. That is why nothing has changed,
but it is also why I am still alive. A contradiction. Is
life better than this, though?*

*God, anybody, help me, please. I am unworthy of
any grace, but help me. I kneel and raise my hands to
the sky and cry for help. My soul cries out from the
well of my destitution.*

Reflections

The painful feeling of self-worthlessness is like no other emotional
pain. When you're feeling it, there is almost nothing you can say to
yourself to make yourself feel better because you don't like yourself
enough to *want* to make yourself feel better. It is an incredibly vicious
and frightening self-inflicted circle of pain. Surprisingly, the solution is often to just bear it, get through it, ask for help and guidance
from trusted adults or doctors, and have faith that those feelings will
eventually go away.

Rejection by the opposite sex can hurt just as much as any kind
of bullying—and more—because it is extremely personal, harsh, and
absolute. There is no gray area for interpretation when someone looks at
you with obvious disgust and then walks away. If you are already feeling
unsure of yourself and struggling with low self-esteem, it can make you
feel as though all your happiness and hopefulness have been ripped out
of you and thrown away. The first time it happens, the pain can be so
intense and unfamiliar that you might think it will never go away.

How can you get through it and survive these feelings? First, and
once again, remember that you are not alone—everyone has faced
rejection unless they live in a society of arranged marriages. Ask your
friends or your parents how many times they were rejected by the
opposite sex. You'll find that they have felt the same painful feelings

more than once before. Second, always remember this: *rejection only means you haven't found the right person yet.* Somewhere in the world is the right person for you. Unfortunately, it can be like searching for a needle in a haystack—you have to search through a lot of chaff before you find what you're looking for.

In Chapters 10 and 12, I talk about how I got past these painful feelings of rejection, how I healed, and how I was able to forgive. I hope these chapters will help you to do the same.

Your Thoughts

- ✦ Have you ever been hurt by the rejection of someone you thought was a friend? How did it make you feel? Was it easy to brush off?
- ✦ Have you ever rejected someone who asked you out on a date? Were you sensitive in your rejection or were you harsh and uncaring? Did you lie to him or her to try to avoid telling your true feelings? Did lying work, or did you have to keep on lying to hide the previous lie?
- ✦ Have you ever felt that life was not worth living? Was the feeling temporary or did it keep coming back? I once felt that way, too, but I don't anymore. Keep reading this book to see why.

Group Discussion

- ✦ Share your experiences with rejection, both those you received and those you gave. Do you have any regrets about how you handled it? What would you do differently if you had to do it again?
- ✦ Is it possible to reject someone without hurting his or her feelings?

✦ When you read this chapter, were you thinking, "This guy really overreacted. It was just a rejection. What's the big deal? Get over it." What kind of personalities, combined with life experiences, would cause one person to view a rejection as trivial and another to view it as devastating?

✦ Role-play asking someone out and getting rejected. Talk about the feelings of the person being rejected and the one doing the rejecting.

✦ How do you define depression? As a particular feeling or particular words and actions?

✦ Do you think it's always obvious that someone is depressed or can they conceal it?

5

The Roller-Coaster Ride

When you get to the end of your rope, tie a knot and hang on.

—Franklin Delano Roosevelt

For me, depression wasn't a constant state of mind; it was more like a roller-coaster ride. During the last three years of high school, sometimes life was great, and I felt that I had gotten through my depths of despair, but then something would happen to drag me back down again. At times it seemed like the peaks were brief and glorious, and the valleys were long, dark, and frightening.

My good grades in school and the joy I found in band class were the only two remaining sources of self-esteem during those years. I enjoyed the gifts of intelligence and musical ability, perhaps even more because I relied on them for a feeling of self-worth. Most teens dread report card day at school. Not me. I quietly looked forward to it—not out of arrogance or pride, but because it was one of the few times I could really feel good about myself.

On one of those report card days, I remembered being especially happy. I had received almost all As and just one or two Bs. It felt good; I needed the boost. I was upbeat, excited, and joyful. When I got home that day, I bounded up the stairs to my room and turned on some of my favorite music on my stereo. It was time to celebrate.

Shortly after, my dad returned home from work. I left my room, went downstairs with my report card in hand, and walked into the kitchen dining area where he was sitting, already watching television. The days of easy and warm relations with my parents were over. It was the difficult teenage years, and my dad and I were usually at odds with each other. Still, I was excited to show my report card to him. It was one of the few times I could get a compliment and a pat on the back from him.

"I got my report card today, Dad," I said smiling, handing it to him as he turned around in his chair.

He took it, gave it only a fleeting glance, then said, not in a tone of compliment, but in a tone of both indifference and hurtfulness, "That's nice."

He tossed my report card carelessly on the table in front of him. He turned back to watching TV without even looking at me.

Hurt and anger hit me like a wave. I grabbed my report card off the table, ran back up the steps to my bedroom, and slammed the door behind me.

I wanted to rip my report card into shreds. I felt so belittled and humiliated. I put my thumbs and index fingers on the middle of one edge of the report card, tensed my muscles preparing to tear it in half, but then I stopped. A small trace of pride kept me from tearing it to pieces. Instead, I tossed it carelessly on my desk. I laid down on my bed and curled up, not sure if I wanted to cry or scream. I did neither, but I let the emotions fester and boil inside me. I had been robbed of the ounce of happiness I had that day, and I resented my father for stealing it from me.

He had never reacted that way to a report card before, and he never did it again, but it was enough to hurt me, enough to remember. It wasn't just the kids at school, I told myself, *even my dad didn't like me*. It reinforced my feelings of worthlessness. It was as if someone were saying, "What are you doing up here being happy? Get back down to the bottom of that roller coaster where you belong."

Sometimes there were peaks in the roller coaster that were never taken away. My music was one of them. No one ever criticized my instrumental ability or made me feel small about it. I don't know

Depression

What is depression?

Depression is a serious medical illness; it's not something that you have made up in your head. It's more than just feeling "down in the dumps" or "blue" for a few days. It's feeling "down" and "low" and "hopeless" for weeks at a time. Depression is not a sign of personal weakness or a condition that can be willed or wished away. People with a depressive illness cannot just "pull themselves together" and get better.

How do I know whether someone is depressed or not?

Although only a qualified medical professional can make a diagnosis that someone is depressed, the following list of symptoms may help you recognize depression in yourself or a friend. A person suffering from depression may experience or display one or more of the following:

✦ Persistent sad, anxious, or "empty" mood.
✦ Persistent feelings of hopelessness, pessimism, guilt, worthlessness, or helplessness.
✦ Loss of interest or pleasure in hobbies and activities that were once enjoyed.
✦ Decreased energy, fatigue, or feeling "slowed down".
✦ Difficulty concentrating, remembering things, or making decisions.
✦ Insomnia, early-morning awakening, or oversleeping.
✦ Appetite or weight loss or overeating and weight gain.
✦ Thoughts of death or suicide; suicide attempts.
✦ Restlessness and irritability.
✦ Persistent physical symptoms that do not respond to treatment such as headaches, digestive disorders, and chronic pain.

Source

National Institute of Mental Health
http://www.nimh.nih.gov/healthinformation/depressionmenu.cfm

whether it was true or not, but I felt that my fellow musicians in band class respected me, at least in terms of my musical ability. I desperately needed that sense of respect. At times, there was no other source of it.

Concert performances were always a natural high for me. Music moves my soul, and a concert, with all of us dressed in our tuxedo-style, black concert uniforms, playing our souls out through our instruments, was an uplifting, exciting experience. When the instrumentalists of a band or orchestra work together to make a musical score come alive, it is sheer magic.

There was one particular high school band concert that I will always remember. Our grand finale piece was Tchaikovsky's 1812 Overture, possibly one of the most challenging pieces we ever played in concert. We rehearsed and rehearsed in the weeks before the performance. As is probably the case with any live performance, you're never quite sure that you are sufficiently prepared and rehearsed even up to the day of the concert. That edge of uncertainty drives you to excel, to try your best to play as you have never played it before. The inspiration of the music and the magic of the moment drove us to perform beyond our expectations.

Tchaikovsky's 1812 Overture is a dramatic piece of music that paints a picture of the Russian's battle for survival against Napoleon's armies. Through the music, you hear and feel the desperation of the besieged Russians, and finally, when they emerge victorious against Napoleon, you hear bells ringing and cannons blasting.

The musical score actually calls for the firing of cannons at particular places in the finale. To simulate cannons, we planned to have an adult alumnus offstage firing shotgun blanks into a large metal barrel partially filled with sand. We couldn't rehearse the "cannon fire" even during our dress rehearsal, so the actual concert would be the first time we would hear the cannons.

As we played the overture, the music carried us through the prelude, into the dark and desperate days of the siege, then to the grand finale of the symphony. During the finale, representing the Russian victory, the brass instruments were blaring, bell chimes were ringing, drums were pounding, and then the cannon blasts began. At first, all you sensed of the "cannon" blast was a silent, body-thumping concussion. A fraction of a second later you heard a loud bang. We could feel the concussions in our chests and see and smell the acrid smoke drifting onto the stage as we continued playing, trying not to be distracted by it.

It was incredible! I had never before and never since played a symphony that was so alive and dramatic, so moving and so memorable. You could feel the Russian's valiant fight, feel their pain, and celebrate their final, but Pyrrhic, victory.

That concert to me represents everything I love about music and performing it live. Through music, we can feel our joys and sorrows, our triumphs and our failures. It reminds us what it is to be human—not just the things we do and say, but what we feel in our hearts and souls. Other than language, it is the depth and breadth of human emotions that sets us apart from other creatures on this planet. Emotions define our existence in both good and bad ways. Music is a reflection of those emotional depths, a way to experience, relive, and remember. Music is an acoustic reflecting pond for our souls.

Peanuts: © United Feature Syndicate, Inc. Reprinted with permission.

Only two other times during the roughly two-year roller coaster ride could I put the past behind me and try again to approach a girl I liked. One such time was on our band trip to Florida during my junior year. I was feeling much better during that trip, even enthusiastic. It was the first time I had ever been to Florida, the first time I had ever seen palm trees with my own eyes. It was refreshing and invigorating to emerge from the catacombs of a long, cold Wisconsin winter into the Florida sunshine. Palm trees, water, and sunshine—it felt like paradise.

At the end of one of our performances, we had a free night at our hotel's conference and banquet center. It was a large hall, the kind used for wedding receptions. There was music playing; the students were mingling and socializing. It almost had a party atmosphere.

I remember I had my eyes on one of the girls in our band, a sophomore, the past few days of the trip. I'll call her Jenna. She had a beautiful tan, a nice smile, and large, warm brown eyes. I didn't know her, but from watching her with her friends, she seemed to be a decent, friendly, down-to-earth girl, the kind I would really like.

I had either confided this to one of my fellow low-brass players, who I'll call Paul, or it was obvious anyway, because he came over to me during the party and said, "Hey, Chad, why don't you go over and talk to Jenna. Ask her to dance or something. She likes you."

I wasn't completely gullible. The defensive wall of caution I had after my experience with Sheri was still there.

"Yeah, right," I replied sarcastically.

"No, really," Paul insisted. "I just talked to her, and she really likes you. You should go talk with her."

I wasn't sure if he was pulling my leg or not, but he had a very sincere look on his face, the most sincere and caring look I had ever seen him wear, in fact.

"Oh, c'mon," I said doubtfully.

"Go on," he continued. "Go talk to her."

I thought about it for a moment. She was really cute, and I definitely wanted to meet her. Maybe this time things would be different; maybe this time it would go better. After all, we were in Florida; we were having fun. The sunshine and the good music had put me in a very positive and confident mood. I felt good about myself, better than I had in awhile.

"Go on," insisted Paul, giving me a nudge.

I took a deep breath, mentally and physically, and started walking over to where she was on the other side of the very crowded room. The walk was painfully long as I weaved my way through small groups of people. Several times on the way, I almost talked myself out of talking to her. Each step seemed to add another knot to my stomach.

As I got close to her, I saw she was talking with two of her friends. For a moment, I lost my nerve. Why do girls always hang out with groups of other girls? How could I ever talk to her without facing potential embarrassment in front of several people at the same time?

No, I thought, *you can't stop now. All your life you've been shy and afraid to take chances, and you miss out on so much as a result. You have to keep going. Besides, Paul told you it would be OK; it will be safe.*

I kept walking.

"Jenna," I began when I reached the spot where she and her friends stood. "Would you like to dance?"

She didn't say a word. She just looked at me with a look that clearly said, "Who are you, and what makes you think you can talk to me?"

She and her friends stared at me in utter silence. I stared back for a moment in a fog of confusion. It took a few seconds for my mind to switch gears from hopeful expectation to the realization that I had been had. I had been set up, and I had fallen for it.

Still, she said nothing, not a word. She just stared at me with a mixture of disgust and surprise. I slowly looked across the room, searching for Paul, feeling small and incredibly embarrassed. I saw him across the room as he started running away to hide from me. He was laughing and wearing a big smile on his face.

I turned slowly away from Jenna and her friends with my head lowered and walked away. I meandered back to the table where I had been sitting before Paul came to talk with me. I sat down hard and crouched down low, hoping no one would see me.

I felt humiliated, both by Jenna's reaction to me and at being so gullible, but mostly by her reaction. She didn't say, "No thanks," or "Sorry, I'm not interested," or "I don't want to hurt your feelings, but no." I was apparently so undesirable that I didn't even warrant a response. I was so unattractive that I didn't even deserve a smile, a kind word, or even a moment of consideration.

The world was saying to me once more, "What are you doing up here being happy? Get back down where you belong!"

Peanuts: © United Feature Syndicate, Inc. Reprinted with permission.

It took six months or more after the incident with Jenna before I felt ready to approach a girl again, ready to try for love again. I had my eye on a cute girl in the band, one of the woodwind players. I'll call her Anna. She was a sweet girl with freckles and a nice smile. Just like Jenna, she had big, brown, warm eyes. She seemed down-to-earth and decent, not arrogant or stuck up as Jenna turned out to be. She had what I thought was the perfect mixture of appearance and personality.

After Sheri and Jenna, I was gun-shy, to say the least, and I was still struggling with the roller coaster of depression. It was only during the uphill parts of the ride that I even considered approaching a girl and taking a risk again. I was too shy and too sensitive to be able to handle rejection very well. This time, I would do things differently. This time, I would try to find out if she liked me first before taking the risk of another painful rejection. Some boys will have a friend ask for them to find out if a girl likes them. I couldn't bear the embarrassment of telling anyone else about my interest in her. I had to find another way—a completely safe way, a way that I wouldn't get hurt.

I decided the solution to the problem was to start writing secret admirer letters to her to get to know her and let her get to know me. It seemed romantic at the time—a safe, distant way to learn more about her without risking another face-to-face catastrophe.

We exchanged a few letters, anonymously on my part. She seemed to enjoy having a secret admirer who was sending her letters, but she didn't seem too interested in getting to know me via mail. She insisted in every letter that she wanted to know who I was or meet me. Finally, I agreed to meet her, although I wasn't sure yet if she liked me (and how could she with only letters). Through exchanging two more letters, we set up a time and a place to meet: the local McDonald's on a Saturday afternoon (romantic, eh?).

On that day I arrived a few minutes early, just in case, wearing what I told her I would be wearing so she would know who I was. I wanted to get there early in case she arrived ahead of schedule. I didn't want her to think I stood her up.

My stomach was in nervous knots again. I felt too queasy to order anything to eat, so I just sat down. The waiting and the wondering was sheer torture for my fragile self-esteem and my shy, sensitive personality. It was even more nerve wracking than just asking a girl out on a date. How did I get here, in this situation? How had my efforts taken such a terrible twist? What I had originally hoped would be the safest, least risky approach to getting to know Anna had turned out to be the most risky one I could possibly imagine. It was like putting my heart and soul out for public viewing, even public ridicule.

Despite the near panic I felt, I was hopeful and excited. Maybe this was the start of something good, maybe something great—the kind of relationship I had been wanting for so long.

I chose a table near the middle of the restaurant where I could see both entrances on opposite sides of the building, because I wasn't sure which door she would use. I probably looked like a spectator at a tennis match, slowly moving my head from side to side, watching the doors, trying not to miss anything.

Shortly after the agreed-upon time, I turned to look at the left entrance, didn't see her there, and then turned back to the right. At that moment, I saw not Anna but her best friend at the door looking at me. She turned and quickly ran back out the door. As I watched her run past one of the windows, she was holding her hand near her mouth in a mock laughter-stifling gesture, although she wasn't trying very hard to contain her laughter.

Oh, God. Not this. What have I done? Now what do I do?

I don't know for certain, but I was probably red in the face with embarrassment. Why did she have to send in her giggly girlfriend to check me out? If I had wanted to be embarrassed in front of her friend, I could have easily done that by asking her out on a date at school. (You're probably saying to yourself, didn't he see the movie *You've Got Mail?* No, this was years before that movie came out, and I had never seen a movie like that, either, at the time. I didn't know that standard operating procedure in a case like this is to send a friend in first to check out the secret admirer to see if he or she is acceptable or a total dog. I only wish I could go back in time to give myself that little tidbit of information.)

Now what do I do, I thought. I felt like running out of the restaurant as fast as I could to run away from what appeared to be yet another embarrassing and humiliating experience. Still, I wondered if there was a chance. Despite her giggly girlfriend, would Anna like me anyway? Would she be happy to find out I was her secret admirer? I decided to wait a few more minutes to see if she would come inside to meet me anyway.

She never did.

The pain and anguish of the past two years came rushing back again.

You're a freak. You're weird. You are undesirable, unattractive, and unworthy. Even a friend won't go out with you. Even a nice, pretty girl like Jenna is disgusted at the thought of dancing with you. Even a cute, sweet girl like Anna is so appalled at the thought of meeting you that she couldn't bring herself to do it. Even her friend thinks you are laughable.

I went home mortified. To make matters worse, I knew that I would see Anna and her giggly girlfriend every single school day in band class. And Jenna. And Sheri. There was absolutely no way to avoid them or not see them, no way to avoid a daily reminder of the three most embarrassing and humiliating moments of my life.

I resolved to not ask girls for a date anymore, at least not for a very, very long time. Three strikes, and you're out, I figured. I couldn't take the humiliation anymore, and I had no reason to believe it wouldn't be humiliating again the next time I tried.

Reflections

We all experience ups and downs. We all experience events in our lives so embarrassing or humiliating that we wish we could unlive them or go back in time to do them differently, to make different choices or take different paths. You are not alone. The critical choice, however, is how we deal with these experiences. Do we treat each one as a personal failure, labeling ourselves a "loser" or "freak" (as I did), or do we chalk them up as learning experiences and quickly get over them? Calling ourselves a loser or a freak is neither helpful nor healthy. Knowing that everyone has experiences like these helps us to know that "it's not just me."

© Zits Partnership, King Features Syndicate. Reprinted with permission.

If the roller-coaster ride seems to linger longer in the deep valleys than on the peaks, then you need to take an active role in smoothing out your ride by putting things in perspective, forgiving those who hurt you, and seeking help if you can't seem to raise yourself up out of the valleys. The seven strategies described in Part 2 of this book are designed to help you smooth out the ride and see the potential in your life, as well as the potential inside of you.

You deserve a life that has more ups than downs, so be sure to read Part 2. Make your ride through life one you can enjoy, or at least bear, rather than a ride of fear. If you want to smooth out the ride, you have to be an active participant in your own life, not just a willing victim of circumstances.

Your Thoughts

+ Think of an embarrassing moment in your life. Did it involve talking to someone of the opposite sex? Did it involve rejection of one kind or another? How did you deal with it?

+ Can you laugh about your embarrassing moments, or do they still hurt too much? Because we are human, we all do silly or dumb things from time to time. Laughing at ourselves takes some of the sting out of such moments. Give it a try. If you can't, don't worry—I couldn't laugh at myself for a long time either, but now I can.

+ What have been the high points of your own personal roller-coaster ride? What moments have you enjoyed and cherished recently?

Group Discussion

+ Have you ever felt hurt by the actions, or inactions, of your parents? How did you deal with it? Can you forgive them? Why or why not?

+ Is it possible to avoid embarrassing moments like the ones described in this chapter, or is that simply one of the risks of living life? Are there any alternatives?

+ How can we put embarrassing moments in perspective? How can we deal with them?

✦ If you have an embarrassing moment that you're willing to share with the group, do so. Feel free to laugh along with, but not at, the person telling the story. We all do embarrassing things—we can't help it—so we might as well have a good time laughing about it.

6

Peering Down into the Abyss

Giving up is the ultimate tragedy.

–ROBERT J. DONOVAN

It was the most surreal funeral I have ever attended. We were at a funeral home, in a room full of teenagers, all dressed in our Sunday best, some crying, others in numbed silence, all mourning the death of a classmate who had committed suicide, a high school senior I'll call Scott.

I will never forget the strange feeling I had during the service. It was as though some unspoken rule of the universe had been broken, as though it couldn't really be happening, as though it were only a bad dream. My mind raced with "why" questions for which there are no answers. Why did he do it? What was wrong in his life? Why hadn't his depression shown visibly? Did he ask for help? Did anyone listen? How could a nice, friendly guy like Scott commit suicide? How could someone who seemed to have a lot going for him get so depressed that he wanted to end his life?

Then an eerie feeling came over me. I knew the answers to my questions. I knew how it could happen. I knew the hollow, empty feeling of depression. I knew the feeling of utter despair and hopelessness that the emptiness brings. I wondered how close I had come to that dark abyss. I wasn't sure, and that scared the heck out of me.

I remember filing past his open casket, along with all the other teens in attendance. I remember pausing briefly, saying a short prayer, and feeling a big lump in my throat. This isn't how things are supposed to be, I thought. No one's life should end this way: enormous potential, unfulfilled.

Scott's suicide and his funeral left a mark on me. I was moved to write down my feelings, so when I got home from Scott's memorial service, I went to my room and wrote this:

> *January 19*
> *Today was the funeral for Scott, a senior who committed suicide. Yes, it is reality. You saw the pain in the tears of your friends.*
>
> *So now, change must come. Now, today. You don't want that end, you want happiness and peace. So today marks the change toward compassion, openness. You must not hide in your shell anymore. Remember today, so you don't forget! Think about it hard! Think of the pain and unhappiness everyone felt.*
>
> *Don't waste any more of your life by self-imposed unhappiness. It is time to live life, to be free at last.*
>
> *Learn from today and remember the eulogy: "There is always someone, if not thousands, ready to listen and bear your burden with you."*
>
> *Stop your pain and prevent theirs by living. You can love, and you will, if you let it happen.*
>
> *Today is the first day of your life!*

I resolved that day to look on the brighter side of life, not to let myself get so depressed that that could happen to me. Life was too precious and short to let that happen, I reasoned.

Surviving Grief

The death of a classmate, friend, or loved one, whether sudden or expected, can be extremely painful. The emotions can seem overwhelming, and it's easy to feel as though you'll never feel better again. How can you get through that pain? How can you deal with it and feel whole again? Use the following suggestions to help you through the process.

✦ Your feelings are normal. When you're grieving over the loss of someone you cared about, it's both normal and natural to feel angry, confused, frustrated, hurt, lonely, sad or hopeless. You feel that way because you care.

✦ Reach out to friends and family. It's OK to hold hands with your mom or dad, ask for a hug from a friend or parent, or just sit and talk one-on-one with someone you love. The comfort we can give each other during a time of loss is one of the greatest gifts of healing we can ever receive.

✦ It's OK to smile and laugh. You don't have to feel sad continuously to honor those who have passed. When we grieve, we might feel like laughing one minute and crying the next. That's normal. Don't be embarrassed or ashamed of your mood swings.

✦ Your pain will lessen with time. It may be hard to believe, but it's true. Don't feel guilty if you find yourself feeling happy again or wanting to resume your normal activities. Those feelings don't dishonor your friend or loved one. You still care about them; you are just healing.

✦ Write in a journal. As you can see in this chapter, I used journaling as a way to deal with grief and emotional pain. Use your journal or even a blank piece of paper to write down your thoughts and feelings. Let out your pain on the paper and feel free to explore some of the big "why" questions of life: "Why do bad things happen?" "Why am I so sad?" Journaling can help you to feel more in control, and you might even find some answers to your questions in the process.

✦ Go for a walk, meditate, or pray. Sometimes finding solitude and time to think or pray can help us to understand what happened, acknowledge and understand our own feelings, and find inner peace.

✦ Ask for help if you need it. If none of these suggestions are helping you through your grief, ask for help from a parent, relative, counselor, youth group leader or other trusted adult. We all need a helping hand at some point in our lives.

I thought about Scott a lot over the next week. Although I didn't know him very well, I had known him since seventh grade when he and I were science lab partners everyday. We had been placed at the same lab table because our last names were alphabetically close together. We hadn't had much contact since seventh grade, but we still said "Hi" to each other in the hallways or in classes. He was a real person to me, not just a name or a face. His absence in the hallways was noticeable and disturbing to me. I wished I could say "Hi" to him again.

My resolve faded some over time, as I soon found myself back where I was, still unsure about myself and unsettled about my life and who I was. But the memory of Scott was always with me, reminding me where I didn't want to go.

Only a few weeks after Scott's funeral, as my parents, sister, and I were sitting at our kitchen table eating breakfast at about 6:30 a.m. on a school day, the phone rang. The four of us briefly stared at each other, not because we wondered who was going to interrupt their breakfast to answer the phone, but because we all knew that a phone call at 6:30 in the morning couldn't be good news.

My mom got up, walked down the hallway toward the front door, and picked up the phone. We could hear her, faintly, from the kitchen.

"Hello? Yes . . . Oh no, not that . . . Oh my . . . OK, thanks for calling." Then she hung up the phone. The three of us were silent as she walked back to the kitchen. My stomach was already in knots. I knew something bad had happened. My mom sat back down at the table, and we all looked at her without saying anything.

"That was someone from the principal's office," she began. "They've started a phone chain to call all of the teachers in the district, so they all know, in case there are questions." She paused, turning to me. "There's been another suicide, another senior in your class, Chad. It was Shawna [name changed]."

My first reaction was anger. Why did we have to go through this again? Wasn't one suicide enough? Didn't anyone notice the signs that it was coming? Wasn't there some way to prevent this? Why does this keep happening?

"Did you know her?" my mom asked.

"Yes . . . but not very well," I replied. "She played a woodwind instrument in band. She sat in the row in front of me, down a few seats."

"Do you want to talk about it? About what you're feeling?" my mom asked.

"I don't know what I'm feeling right now," I said. "I'm kind of numb right now."

I went to school that day feeling angry, distant, sad, and mournful. I didn't know Shawna very well, but I saw her every day in band class, and we spoke occasionally. She seemed to be a nice, friendly girl. She was quiet, but she had friends; she was likable. Her empty seat that day in band class stood out unmistakably and disturbingly. Selfishly, I was glad that I wasn't one of the two people who had to sit next to her empty chair during class.

That afternoon, the entire senior class, roughly 250 of us, was sent to the auditorium for what we suspected was some kind of counseling session. It was the same auditorium where our band concerts were held, but this time I was in the audience instead of on stage. Our class filled the auditorium. There was low chatter and even some quiet laughter in the room, the kind of laughter teens have when they feel nervous or anxious about a situation that makes them feel uncomfortable. Everyone quieted down when the principal walked up onto the stage.

"I suppose all of you have an idea why you are here today," he began. "We wanted to clear up any questions you might have and let you know about counseling that is available.

"With me today is Dave Sorens [name changed] from the county Department of Mental Health Services. He has a few things to say about the county's services and counseling." He motioned to Mr. Sorens who was standing at stage left and introduced him by simply saying, "Mr. Sorens."

Mr. Sorens traded places with the principal, centering himself on the stage, and then began talking to us.

"Suicide is no laughing matter," he said with a very serious expression on his face. "Two suicides in one school is two too many.

"I want you to know that there is help available if you need it. If you're feeling depressed, feeling like you might want to take your

Helping a Friend—Intervention

"I think my friend is depressed, maybe even suicidal. What should I do?"

If you think your friend is very depressed, maybe even suicidal, use the following guidelines to help you know how to get involved (intervene) to prevent a suicide.

✦ Learn the signs and symptoms of depression and suicidal behavior. For more information see the Chapter 5 sidebar "Signs and Symptoms of Depression," the "Suicidal Behavior" sidebar in this chapter, and the Resources section at the end of this book. It is *not* your job to be a psychologist for your friend, but the information in these resources might help you to recognize a situation that requires intervention (getting involved).

✦ Have the confidence to get involved. Remember, actions speak louder than words, so your friend might say he or she is fine, but if his or her actions indicate depression or suicidal thoughts, then pay attention to them. Have the confidence to tell a trusted adult what you have seen, what you have heard, or how your friend's actions have changed.

✦ Try to anticipate how your friend may be feeling. Talk with your friend. Be a good listener. Put yourself in your friend's shoes so you can be sensitive and understanding toward him or her. Think about the emotions your friend may or may not be feeling and what might have caused these feelings.

✦ Tell your friend it is important to get help. Often a person who is feeling overwhelmed or out of control isn't able to recognize he or she needs help and see that help is available and within reach.

✦ Ask your friend to make a plan for getting help from one of the many resources in your community: a parent, an aunt or uncle, older siblings, a youth group leader, a favorite teacher or coach, a coworker, a neighbor, a guidance counselor, or a crisis hotline. Agree on the day and time that your friend will talk to you again about who was contacted.

✦ Recognize that you may need help too. Helping someone else takes a lot of energy. Don't expect yourself to be able to handle it all on your own. Be aware of your personal limits and abilities and know that it's okay to go to an adult for additional help.

> ✦ NEVER promise to keep a plan of suicide a secret. Keeping it a secret will never help your friend. Tell your friend you value life over friendship and are prepared to do whatever it takes to help him or her.
>
> **Source**
>
> KUTO, Kids Under Twenty One
> http://www.kuto.org/prevention/intervention.html

life, then by all means get some help. You can talk with guidance counselors, teachers, or clergy. You can call the Department of Mental Health Services. We have crisis counselors who can help anytime, day or night. You can even call me personally if you want to. I'll be handing out my business card when you leave today. That's what I'm there for. The most important thing to remember is to ask for help."

He paused briefly, partly for effect I think, and partly to let what he said soak in.

"Now," he began again, "if you have any questions about suicide or what help is available through the Department of Mental Health Services, you can ask those questions now."

He surveyed the room to see if any hands were raised. None were. The room was completely silent. I looked to both sides to see if anyone would start raising their hands, but so far there was no movement.

Teens don't like to ask pointed, personal questions in such a large group. They're afraid of standing out or sounding dumb. I was no different, but my mind was full of questions. I tried to think of a question that wouldn't give away my own struggle with mild depression that I had kept well hidden.

"C'mon, now," said Mr. Sorens, breaking the silence. "There must be some questions."

I looked around the auditorium again, but still there were no raised hands. Frustrated, and irritated with having to stand out on my own, I raised my hand.

"Yes?" Mr. Sorens said, calling on me.

"Um . . . what should you do if you know someone who's depressed?" I asked.

"The most important thing to do is to encourage them to talk with a counselor or teacher, or even call me," he answered. "Or, you could tell a counselor that you have a friend who is depressed, and he or she can talk to your friend.

"Any other questions?" he asked the audience.

Was that it? Was that all he was going to say? I wanted to hear something that would help me right then and there. I wanted to know some strategies for getting through what I had been going through. I wanted to hear encouragement, support, hope. I didn't want to hear what to me was a pat answer.

Someone else must have raised a hand, because Mr. Sorens pointed and said, "Yes, over there."

"How did Shawna die?" came the question from someone I couldn't see. Mr. Sorens briefly, in one sentence, answered the question.

"Any other questions?" Mr. Sorens asked. The room was silent once again, and no other hands were raised.

After a few more silent, awkward seconds, our principal walked to center stage to join Mr. Sorens. "This is your chance to ask questions," he said. Still no hands were raised. The seniors looked around at each other to see if anyone else would.

"If there aren't any other questions, I'd like to thank Mr. Sorens for being here today," the principal said. "He will be available the rest of today, in the office, if you have questions or want to talk about what has happened." We were then dismissed to go back to our classes.

That was it. Two teens were dead, and we got a little one-minute lecture on getting help. In my opinion, it was far too little, far too late. No one had bothered to talk with us about suicide and depression until *after* two teens were dead. Even then, they didn't really talk with us. They had 250 teens in the room, a captive audience to whom they could have spoken about the signs of depression, dealing with depression, how to get through the teen years and deal with the loss of a friend—but they didn't. They had the opportunity, and they blew it. I walked out of the auditorium fuming.

I doubt many of my classmates went to see Mr. Sorens or our counselors that day. I know I didn't. Like a typical teenager, I felt too embarrassed to get help. I was even afraid someone would see me walking to the office to get help. Also, like most boys, and most men, I felt I could handle the situation myself. Dealing with it on my own felt like a sign of strength; asking for help, like asking for directions, was a sign of weakness. Teens—both boys and girls—typically don't like to ask for information, so you have to give it to them. I wish the counselors and principal had recognized that and taken the opportunity to not just talk to, but also educate, the entire group of seniors that day. I desperately needed to hear words of encouragement, hope, and advice.

Shawna's funeral was held at a large church, with family, friends, and classmates attending the same service. Whether it was because adults were present or because, unfortunately, I was beginning to get used to funeral services, the service didn't seem as surreal and otherworldly as Scott's had. It still felt odd and uncomfortable, though, to go to the funerals of two of my teenage classmates within a few weeks of each other. It still felt like it shouldn't be happening. It still left a dark memory in my mind that will be there for the rest of my life.

Reflections

Scott and Shawna's suicides disturb me even more today as an adult than they did during high school. Now I know what they lost; now I know what they threw away. I weep for their eyes that will never look into the eyes of their first, and only, true love. I weep for their hands that will never feel the soft, gentle caress when holding their young child's hand. I weep for their ears that will never hear the squeal of delight from their son or daughter who is happy that Mommy or Daddy is home from work. I weep for their hearts that will never melt when they hear their child say, "I love you, Daddy," or "I love you, Mommy."

I weep for all of these things and more, for all of the wonderful and joyful moments in life that I have experienced since then, moments

Suicidal Behavior

The warning signs and risk factors shown here may help you identify suicidal behavior in a friend. No suicidal person will display all of these behaviors, but a combination of them may mean your friend is at risk for suicide. If you think your friend is suicidal, urge him or her to contact one of the suicide prevention hotlines listed in the Resources section at the end of this book.

Warning Signs of Suicide
+ Abrupt changes in personality.
+ Giving away personal possessions.
+ A previous suicide attempt.
+ Use of drugs or alcohol.
+ Change in eating pattern—significant weight change.
+ Change in sleeping pattern—insomnia/oversleeping.
+ Unwillingness or inability to communicate.
+ Depression.
+ Extreme or extended boredom.
+ Unusual carelessness (accident prone).
+ Unusual sadness, discouragement, and loneliness.
+ Thoughts of death, suicide, or wishing to be dead, planning a funeral.
+ Neglecting school work or personal appearance.
+ Running away from home or skipping school.
+ Rebelliousness—reckless behavior.
+ Withdrawal from people or activities they love
+ Confusion—inability to concentrate.
+ Chronic pain, panic, or anxiety.
+ Perfectionism.
+ Restlessness.

Risk Factors for Suicide
+ Problems with school or the law.
+ Breakup of a romance or a harsh rejection.
+ Unexpected pregnancy.
+ A stressful family life, including having parents who are depressed or are substance abusers or a family history of suicide.

- ✦ Loss of security or fear of authority, peers, group, or gang members.
- ✦ Stress due to new situations; college or relocating to a new community; divorce.
- ✦ Failing in school or failing to pass an important test.
- ✦ A serious illness or injury.
- ✦ Seriously injuring another person or causing another person's death (example: automobile accident).
- ✦ Any personally traumatic event.
- ✦ Major loss of a loved one, a home, a relationship.
- ✦ Drug addiction.

Sources

The Yellow Ribbon International Suicide Prevention Program
http://www.yellowribbon.org/

American Foundation for Suicide Prevention
http://www.afsp.org/

that they will never experience, never savor and enjoy as I have. I am absolutely certain they would have experienced all these things—and more—if they had hung on a little longer. They were almost at the finish line, almost to the beginning of the best part of their lives.

Henriette Ann Klauser wrote in her book *Write It Down, Make It Happen* (Touchstone, 2001) about a gold miner named Mr. Darby who mined in Colorado during the Gold Rush days. He dug and dug looking for gold until he had exhausted his money and his spirit. He gave up, sold his mine to another miner, and went home. The new owner struck gold only *three feet* from where Mr. Darby had given up digging. Scott and Shawna stopped three feet from the gold, too. They were less than five months from high school graduation, only five months from the gold of a new and better life. It frightens me to think how close I might have been to giving up as well. I'm glad I didn't.

I wish I could talk with Scott and Shawna now, reaching back into the past, to tell them what I know, what I've experienced and learned in my life. It's as though they are dangling over a cliff, clinging by their fingertips to a narrow ledge far below me. I reach down trying to help them, calling out to them, "Hang on! Just hang on a little bit longer! Things will get better. Trust me. Please . . . please . . . just trust me! Hang on!"

It's too late. They can't hear me anymore.

But you can.

Don't give up. Never give up on your life, no matter how hard, dark, or messy it gets. Keep hanging on, because something has to change. Life never stays the same way for very long. Don't give up; you're only three feet from the gold!

Your Thoughts

✦ Have you ever known someone who committed suicide? How did it make you feel? What do you think they've missed in life because they weren't able to hold on?

✦ Get out a sheet of paper and put the following title at the top: "Fifty Things to Live For." On that sheet, make a list of fifty good things that make life worth living or things to look forward to as you become an adult. Maybe it's having a Super Bowl party with your friends, or falling in love, or getting a college degree, or anything else that brings you joy and satisfaction. Once you get started, you'll find it's easy to make a list. After you've completed your list, keep it in a safe place and read it often. When you do, you'll see that despite life's ups and downs, there are many reasons to enjoy and cherish your life.

Group Discussion

✦ Why are teens, and even many adults, so afraid to ask for help with their mental health?

✦ Why is there a stigma associated with depression? Should there be? Is it the depressed person's fault that he or she is depressed?

✦ Do you know the signs and symptoms of depression? Would you recognize them in a friend? In yourself? Research the signs and symptoms of depression (look at the sidebar in this chapter and in the Resources section at the end of this book). Discuss them as a group.

✦ What could society do to change views about depression? As an exercise for your group, develop a detailed plan for an education and awareness campaign about mental health and teen depression.

✦ Despite perpetually tight budgets, what could school districts do to educate young people about the signs of depression? How can they help teens to get help and survive? What can be done to *prevent* teen suicides?

✦ Does your school have any suicide prevention programs? If not, why do you think they don't? Discuss these approaches to suicide prevention: Silence (not putting the idea of suicide in young people's minds) or active education (teaching young people to recognize depression and seek treatment).

✦ You won't fully understand this until you are a parent yourself, but the death of your own child is the most painful, most unimaginable thing you could ever have to bear. It is such an unthinkable thought that most parents drive it out of their minds, refusing to even bring up the subject of suicide with their children. What would you say to an adult to convince them to talk with their children about depression and suicide prevention?

7
Coming into the Light

The lowest ebb is the turn of the tide.

—Henry Wadsworth Longfellow

The roller-coaster ride of depression didn't stop all at once. There was no epiphany, no life-changing moment. It was slow and gradual, but it was enough to be noticeable.

The change became most noticeable during my senior year of high school, a year that brought some welcome changes and new challenges. Best of all, the bullies were gone. The bullies in my class had dropped out of school before their senior year, those who were a year older than me had graduated, and the underclassmen had enough respect for the seniors that they weren't a problem either. I was bully-free for the first time since sixth grade, and it felt great!

I was also maturing, beginning to gain at least a little more confidence and self-esteem, but still struggling with both. Gym class was improving, too, not because I was more coordinated or stronger, but because the juniors and seniors were given at least two choices of physical education units each semester. I could choose activities in which I would at least not feel embarrassed and possibly even hold my own. I chose soccer over baseball, cross-country skiing over basketball, bicycling over track.

I don't know whether the improvement in my life was more the result of these outside, out-of-my-control changes or the conscious decision I made after Scott's suicide to keep slogging through the muck in life no matter what. It was probably a mix of both of these, but my decision to keep going certainly made it possible to *get* to the point in my life where positive changes were occurring.

The fact that it was my senior year gave me even more to be excited about—I was only a year away from college, to which I looked forward with great anticipation. College was like a bright shining beacon in the future—a chance to excel in an area of my choosing, a chance to be challenged intellectually, and a chance to be with people who had similar interests and goals. Looking to the future with hope helped to lift my spirits throughout my senior year.

Another welcome change was that, for better or worse, I had given up on the idea of asking a girl out on a date, at least until after high school or until I was absolutely sure the girl wanted to go out with me. It had been too painful and emotionally crippling each time I was rejected cruelly without even a moment of consideration. My fragile self-esteem couldn't take it anymore, so I gave up trying.

I remember taking a high school psychology class in which we learned about mice or rats in a maze trained with food or electrical shocks to chose the "right" path through the maze. Life felt a lot like that to me. I decided not to be a stupid mouse that continued receiving the painful electrical shock each time he tried the "wrong" path. I could learn, I told myself, but I felt like a stupid human because it probably took me just as many shocks as the mouse received before I learned my lesson.

Ironically, my decision to give up asking girls for a date increased my sense of peace and contentment, but it also increased my sense of loneliness and despair at ever finding someone who would love me for who I was. On the one hand, it was a relief, but on the other hand it made companionship and love seem further away than ever before.

There was one girl, a friend of mine I'll call Tonya, for whom I briefly considered breaking my self-imposed "don't ask anyone out on a date" rule. She had wavy brown hair that hung just past her shoulders, warm brown eyes, and the face of a porcelain doll. She was warm and caring, sweet and humble, honest and decent. She was remarkably similar to the woman I would someday marry.

Tonya was someone I could talk with and whose company I enjoyed. I once even rode my bike five or six miles to her house to visit with her and talk out some of my hurt, anxious, and angry teenage feelings. She was a good listener and a good friend.

That's exactly why I never asked her out on a date. I valued her friendship too much to risk it by asking her out, too much to chance losing another friend as I did with Sheri. Losing her friendship would have been painful and personal. More important, being rejected by someone I held in such high esteem would have been devastating. I couldn't imagine going through that, so I made sure I wouldn't have to. Still, the fact that she liked being my friend boosted my self-esteem and made me feel more worthy of self-respect.

During the last few months of my senior year, as graduation was approaching, my thoughts were on the future and college. It felt like I was finally going to be free, not from my parents as many teens feel, but free to begin an exciting and intellectually challenging new life. I was—and still am—a dreamer, and going off to college meant the beginning of pursuing my dreams.

As the finish line of graduation approached, I cared even less and less about dating. As often happens in life, when you stop worrying about something, that's when it comes to you. While helping with the drama club's set construction, I met a high school junior girl. She made it very apparent that she wanted me to ask her out on a date. At first, I wasn't sure I wanted to ask her out. She was cute and bubbly, and I liked her, but I only felt a mild spark of interest. In retrospect I should have trusted my gut instincts, but it felt so good to have a girl who I liked finally express an interest in me and to genuinely like me for who I was that I asked her out on a date. My first official date of my life was in March of my senior year of high school—less than three months before graduation.

With college starting, and steadily dating a girlfriend, you would have thought my roller-coaster ride was over, but it wasn't. My first semester of college turned out to be a continuously bumpy ride. My relationship with my girlfriend was on-again, off-again. It didn't help that I was going to college about an hour and a quarter drive away (I rode a bus home on most weekends), and she was still in high school. Increasingly apparent differences in our personalities, plus the distance, meant our relationship went up and down all the time. I was so afraid of being alone, so afraid that I would fall back into hopelessness and depression, that I hung on to the relationship far longer than I should have. We liked each other and enjoyed each other's company, but that wasn't enough; we just weren't meant for each other.

The college front wasn't going very well either. I was a shy, quiet teen attending a huge university (roughly 50,000 total undergraduate and graduate students) after growing up in a small town with a sheltered life. I was lost in the crowd. I couldn't find and make friends. Leaving the campus each weekend to go home didn't help that either, I suppose.

As if feeling lost in the crowd and having a rough relationship weren't enough, I was also seriously struggling with what I thought would be my major area of study: physics and astronomy. I dropped out of physics one month into my first semester of college. By the end of my first semester I had dropped out of school entirely and moved back home.

There I was, a formerly straight-A student, the person my fellow high school seniors voted most likely to become a scientist, dropping out of college after only one semester. I felt like a failure, a total washout. I didn't know what I wanted to do. I didn't know where, or if, I wanted to continue college. My parents weren't understanding of my struggle, either. They made comments like, "I don't know how, but somehow we've failed as parents." It made me really angry when they said that, not because I couldn't appreciate how they felt, but because I desperately needed help, support, guidance, and encouragement, not criticism.

Like the turning point in a novel, however, my true and best life was just around the corner. I only had to hang on a little longer. Although I didn't know it at the time, I was just three feet from the gold.

My parents convinced me to enroll in the spring semester at one of our state university's two-year centers a few miles away from our house. I could live at home to save money, and I wouldn't be losing an entire semester. The courses I would take there would transfer to one of the larger state schools where I could finish out a degree, whatever that might eventually be.

That semester I took a class in computer programming, using the BASIC programming language on the original IBM personal computers. I ate it up. I couldn't get enough of it; I absolutely loved it. Halfway through that semester, I knew that writing computer software was what I really wanted to do for my career. My sense of excitement and hope for the future returned. I finally felt that I had direction again.

My newfound love of computer programming was ironic, though. In high school, I had taken a one-semester course in computers and programming during my senior year, the first computer course ever taught at my high school. I'm not sure if it was a poor curriculum or the fact that the teacher was learning about computers along with us, but I came away from that class vowing that I would never work with computers. It took dropping out of college—which seemed like a tremendous failure at the time—to set up the situation in which I could find out what I really wanted to do with my life. If I hadn't dropped out of that first school, I don't know when, or if, I would have discovered my interest in computer programming. Life is often like that: Circumstances that seem painful, discouraging, and out of our control often lead us down a path that we later realize we wouldn't change for the world.

During that semester, my relationship with my girlfriend became even more on-again, off-again. Near the end of that floundering relationship I met another girl, Heidi, through mutual friends at our church.

Heidi was special. I knew that right away even though she was dating a friend of mine, who also went to our church. We saw each other only once a week, at church, when we sat with our group of about seven friends. Sometimes we sat near each other, other times we were on opposite ends of the pew, but even then she leaned forward to look down the pew to give me a smile and a hello when I sat down. I still remember the way her face lit up when she saw me. Wow! I know my face lit up, too, when I saw her. She had short brown hair, brown eyes, and a pretty face. I recall thinking, how did my friend find such a wonderful girl? Why couldn't I be so lucky?

Later that spring, my girlfriend and I were really on the rocks, bordering on breakup. Heidi had recently broken up with her boyfriend, so I knew she was someone with whom I could talk about what I was going through. I also liked her a lot. I think subconsciously my brain was pointing me in the right direction, despite the rest of my brain clinging to the familiarity of a known, yet failing, relationship. I asked Heidi for her phone number, saying I wanted to talk with her sometime. She gave it to me right away.

Only a few weeks later, my girlfriend and I officially broke up. A few days after that, I gave Heidi a call, not just to talk, but to ask her out on a date. How could I take the risk again? Wasn't I afraid of rejection? Well, Heidi was already a friend, and she was such a warm and gentle person that I figured if she did reject me, it would probably be the kindest and sweetest rejection I would ever hear. I never had to find out, though, because she said "yes."

Heidi and I hit it off right away. There was something about her that was just right. She was similar in appearance to the other girls I had been interested in before, but she was even cuter, nicer, more sincere, easy going, and down-to-earth than they were.

At first, I was afraid that our mutual attraction was a result of both of us being on the rebound from recent dating breakups, but our relationship felt so right, so natural, that I soon realized rebound didn't have anything to do with it. She was the one.

That summer, between my freshman and sophomore years at college, everything finally came together for me. I had found myself, found what I wanted to do with my life, and found the person I wanted to spend that life with. It was the beginning of what I call my true and best life.

Reflections

Some of the best and most memorable years of my life followed that summer: continuing to fall in love, finishing college and getting a degree, our wedding, my first job, new friends, buying our first home, getting my master's degree, and having our two children. My life since that summer has been blessed beyond anything I had hoped to receive or deserve.

There are no bullies in my life now, either. I can associate with people I enjoy, make the friends *I* want to make, choose the jobs *I* want to have. Heidi and I can make our own choices for how we want to live our lives, and believe me, that kind of freedom, while it has its challenges and uncertainties, is a lot of fun! There is definitely something to be said for reaching adulthood.

You and your life *will* change! Your appearance will change, your attitudes and interests will change, and your perspective on life will change after high school. Chances are, you will also be more confident and self-assured and will feel more respected than when you were in high school. Life has surprises in store for you, some that you cannot even imagine or believe right now. So don't give up hope as a teen or preteen. Don't stop three feet from the gold. You haven't opened the gifts of your true and best life yet.

When I was a teenager, I didn't believe I would ever be happy or have what I wanted in life. There were times when I didn't even believe I deserved happiness. But look at me now. I have a wife who loves both me and our children so much and so honestly that she has taught me the meaning of unconditional love. I have children who love me for who I am. They love me so much that they miss me even if I'm gone for one day. Not bad for a guy who used to believe no one could ever love him. I've had supervisors in my career who valued my dedication and talents so much that they joked about cloning a few dozen copies of me. Not bad for a guy who once thought he was worthless.

I'm not telling you these things for vanity's sake or to brag. I'm telling you so that you will know how completely different your life might turn out from how you imagine it turning out right now. Go back and read some of my writings from the years when I was depressed and then compare them to how I describe myself and my life today. I can't promise your life will change as dramatically as mine has, but it most definitely *will* change!

Make a commitment to yourself to survive your teen and preteen years so that you can discover the gifts that are waiting for you in adulthood. Like me, you might be pleasantly surprised.

Your Thoughts

+ What might be the turning point in your life? When do you think it could happen? What answers or resolutions to problems would define the turning point for you?
+ Negative thoughts about the future are self-defeating and often self-fulfilling. Imagine, and maybe even write down in story form, your dream for a positive turning point in your life.
+ Has anyone made hurtful or discouraging comments to you at a time of failure in your life? What might be the reasons behind their comments? A sense of responsibility for your moment of failure? Empathy? Understanding the reasons can change your perspective and take the sting out of their words.

Group Discussion

✦ What are the life events or experiences that you believe will provide fulfillment, emotional completion and meaning to your life? Some examples might be getting a college degree, owning a business, falling in love, buying your first home, having children, pursuing a certain career, writing a book, conquering an illness or addiction, winning a championship medal in an athletic event, or achieving financial success.

✦ Are the sources of life fulfillment the same for everyone? Does it matter that the things you most desperately need in your life might not matter at all to a friend of yours or maybe even your parents? Are those differences in life expectations a source of stress and strain for you? Why or why not?

✦ Why is it so hard for us to believe someone who says, "Your life will get better, just wait and see"? Taking helpful advice purely on faith isn't easy; it's natural to want proof. What evidence is there around you to prove this advice, even if you don't see that evidence in your own life?

Part 2: Seven Ways

8

Seven Ways to Survive and Thrive

If you want to see the sun shine, you have to weather the storm.

—FRANK LANE

What experiences have damaged your self-esteem? Was it classmates who laughed at you in gym class when your attempt to shoot a basket fell many feet short of the hoop? Or was it your father saying you couldn't be his son because you are such a weakling and a wimp? Was it your drunken parent who hit you and told you that you were worthless? Or was it the popular kids who called you "fatso" and other names? Was it a teacher who said nothing at all, but gave you a look of pity or disgust when he handed back your term paper with a grade of D?

The reasons we loose our self-esteem are as numerous and unique as each individual's own experiences, but the results are the same: We hurt and we think less of ourselves. If we let them, over time these repeated and recurring painful events start to take a permanent toll on our self-esteem.

The good news is you can survive, even thrive, despite these painful events, and begin to repair the damage to your self-esteem using the seven strategies described in the remainder of this book: forgiveness, understanding, perspective, faith, gifts and talents, involvement, and hopes and dreams.

1. **Forgiveness.** Forgiving isn't just the "right thing to do," it is the beginning of our own healing—our emotional healing. Truly forgiving involves letting go of anger and resentment. It means leaving negative emotions and thoughts behind us forever.

2. **Understanding.** Only by trying to understand the people who hurt us—their motivations, their reasons, and their own pain—can we begin to put their actions in perspective, free ourselves from the feeling that their cruelty is our fault, and take the first steps down the path of forgiveness.

3. **Perspective.** Putting our situation and our life in perspective lessens the hurtful actions of others and gives us the hope we need to persevere. Perspective can reduce mountains of painful moments back down to the molehills they should be.

4. **Faith.** If you have a religious faith, it can be one of the greatest sources of strength and peace you will ever have. It can give you hope at a time in your life when you need it most.

5. **Gifts and Talents.** Knowing you have a gift or talent for something can boost your self-esteem and your self-concept. Exploring your talents and challenging yourself to excel builds character, hope, and confidence.

6. **Involvement.** Get involved! Being a member of a youth organization—any kind of youth organization—is a great way to make friends and develop a healthy sense of belonging. It also gives you a lot less time to dwell on the negatives in your life, less time to wallow in self-pity.

7. **Hopes and Dreams.** Deep in our hearts, deep in our souls, we are all dreamers. Our dreams and hopes for the future can be a bright, shinning light guiding us through the rocky shoals of our lives.

These seven ways of coping and surviving are realistic strategies. I know they are, because they are strategies I used to help me get through my adolescent years. Except for a few that I realized in adulthood, most were tried and tested from age eleven to eighteen.

The seven strategies are also concrete and tangible. If you're like me, platitudes about the difficult teenage years, like "It's just part of growing up," or "Don't worry, you'll get through it," don't help much. I needed more than simple sayings and platitudes to deal with the challenges I faced during my teen and preteen years.

Each of the following chapters is devoted to the seven strategies. You don't need to read them in any particular order, but it helps to have read Part 1 of this book first, because I refer to examples from my own personal experience. Although order isn't important, I encourage you to read all seven chapters because you won't know which strategies will help you the most until you've read each of them and considered how you can apply them to your own life.

You'll notice as you read this section that forgiveness and understanding are combined into one tightly interwoven strategy that takes three chapters to discuss. The two strategies are closely intertwined (it's difficult to achieve one without the other), so I discuss them together. These two strategies are also so broad that you could write an entire book about them, but for the purpose of this book, the focus is on forgiving your peers, your parents, and yourself.

Although negative experiences can affect us at any time in our lives, they are particularly hurtful and damaging during our teen and preteen years—right at the time when we are desperately searching for and forming our own identity and our sense of self. It's as though our self-image is a ball of clay being molded and formed, then Wham!, that ball of clay is flattened by a huge fist. Everything we thought we were changes, and if we're not careful, that ball of clay will never regain its former shape.

Once the teenage years were over, it took me years to reshape my self-concept and to remold that clay in a more positive way. Speaking as the voice of experience, I can say this: Don't let the negative events during your teen and preteen years flatten your self-concept. I know, that's easier said than done, but I also know you have more power to maintain your self-concept than you might think. That's what Part 2 of this book is all about: remembering and building a self-image that is positive, a self-image that you *deserve* to have. Part 2 is also about hope: hope for your future. Your real and best life is waiting for you in adulthood, waiting to be opened, discovered, and experienced.

If the strategies I discuss in this section don't work for you, invent your own or ask for help from a professional such as a guidance counselor, clergy, or psychologist. Right now, you're probably saying, "Hey, you said you didn't want to ask for help when you were a teen. You were even afraid to ask for help. Why should I?" In retrospect, I should have asked for more help from counselors or other professionals. Thankfully, I found and used the strategies described in this section to get through it on my own, but I think the task of surviving would have been much easier—and more certain—with some help from a seasoned professional.

Don't be afraid to ask for help like I was. Think about it: If your car needs repairs, and you can't figure out how to fix it yourself, you don't hesitate to take it to a trained mechanic. Why then, should we hesitate to get professional help to improve our mental health and the quality of our lives? If cost is an issue, then consider getting help from school guidance counselors or clergy. There are also free telephone hotlines for support, including suicide prevention (see the Resources section at the end of this book).

Whatever strategies you use, whether they are from this book or from another source, make sure you don't give up. Do what ever you have to do to survive so that you can find out what life has waiting for you, so you can open the gift of your true and best life in adulthood.

Your Thoughts

✦ Before you read the rest of Part 2, think of strategies you might have already used to survive and persevere. Write them down and compare and contrast them to my strategies as you read.

Group Discussion

✦ There is no shortage of books, radio programs, and television shows that try to give you "top ten" lists of ways to improve your life, make more money, or find the perfect mate. Is our society too focused on quick fixes and advice that is well intentioned but lacking in substance?

✦ What does it really take to incorporate new strategies or techniques for living into your life? Is just reading or hearing about them enough? Why or why not?

9

Why Forgiveness and Understanding?

When we know how to read our own hearts,
we acquire wisdom of the hearts of others.

—DENIS DIDEROT

Forgiveness. On the surface, it sounds so easy. You've probably heard many people talk about forgiveness, but it is one of the most difficult things for a person to do. Even people who recognize the power of forgiveness often fall short of achieving it. It's a very tough path to walk.

If forgiving and understanding someone who has hurt you is so difficult, and most people don't do a very good job of it anyway, then why should you bother? Why try? You can probably find many books and magazine articles that attempt to answer these questions, but for me there are two primary reasons to forgive someone. First, it's the right thing to do, and second, forgiveness is the beginning of healing. Your healing.

It's easy to say you forgive someone, but it's quite another thing to actually do it in your heart. Truly forgiving someone requires you to remember the hurt, think it through, and even relive it in your mind to come to an understanding of the people that hurt you and why they did. In other words, you have to put yourself in their shoes. Only then can you forgive them for what they've done and in the process unload the huge burden of pain you have been carrying. You don't necessarily have to forgive them face to face, either (although it would be great if you could). If you honestly and sincerely forgive them in your heart, then the burden will be lifted.

I have to admit that during most of high school, I didn't do too well with forgiveness. Sometimes I was able to achieve understanding—realizing that bullies have their own problems and hang-ups that cause them to behave the way they do—but forgiveness was another thing altogether.

For most of the years since high school, I've tried to forget rather than forgive and understand. It seems like a lifetime ago now, as if I were a different person, and I suppose I was. Given the passage of time, it's far easier to forget than forgive, but forgetting is not the same as forgiving. Forgiveness requires you to remember the hurt before you can begin the process of forgiving.

Forgetting is not the same as forgiving.

The next two chapters focus on three important groups of people to consider forgiving: your peers (other young people who have hurt you in some way), your parents, and yourself. If you can achieve forgiveness for all these people, then you will have freed yourself from a huge emotional burden. Don't worry if you can't forgive instantly or easily. It can take time. It took me many years. Even partial forgiveness, however, can still be very healing.

As you read the next two chapters, have a piece of paper and a pen or pencil ready to jot down notes about people who hurt you. There are blank pages at the end of this book that you can also use to write your notes. Write down your thoughts about how or why you can forgive people, just like the exercises I go through in these chapters.

Writing the following two chapters was probably the most healing part of writing this entire book. When I finished, I felt relieved and happy. I truly felt a burden lifted. I encourage you to write your thoughts down too, to see if you discover the same effect.

Your Thoughts

✦ Do you think forgiving people is necessary, or do you scoff at the idea? Consider *why* you think the way you do about forgiveness. What have your parents, teachers, or clergy taught you about it? Have they influenced your opinion about forgiveness?

Group Discussion

✦ Is the concept of forgiveness primarily a religious theme, or can the theme of forgiveness be found in other places in society? Do television, movies, or books portray forgiveness as a positive or desirable thing? Do they ignore it or minimize it? Provide specific examples.

✦ As an exercise, go to a library or bookstore before your next group meeting. Find all the books on the topic of forgiving people. Write down their titles and who the receiver of forgiveness is supposed to be (reading the back cover is usually sufficient to determine that). Bring your notes to the next group meeting and compare them. Were you surprised by what you found?

10

Forgiveness and Understanding: Your Peers

To carry a grudge is like being stung to death by one bee.

—William H. Walton

While writing this book, I've been forced to confront my memories of my teen and preteen years and the people who caused emotional or physical pain for me during that time. Before writing this book, I never resolved my leftover negative emotions and pain from those years. For the first few years after high school graduation, I was still too angry and hurt to forgive and understand my peers. For a decade after that, I just tried to forget those years, to shove them to the back of my mind where the memories didn't bother me. But if forgiveness is the beginning of healing, you can't just forget, or the wounds can never truly heal.

In this chapter, I walk you through my own personal journey of forgiving my peers, a journey I didn't take until I wrote this chapter. As you read, think about the teens and preteens who hurt you: friends, classmates, neighbors, or others. Try to see them, by analogy, in the people I've described from my experiences. See if you can walk through your own journey of forgiveness along with me.

Let's start with Jed, my first bully. He was probably the bully who showed the most remorse for beating me up. I'm not talking about his crying in the principal's office—that was out of fear for himself. Rather, I'm talking about how he treated me after the fight. He never apologized, as such, but he did seem genuinely sorry, and he made a point of asking how I was doing the next day. Whatever cruel sense of joy or triumph he might have felt during the fight, it evaporated quickly. He felt sorry for what he had done.

I think Jed felt pressured to fight, too. He had sidekicks, just as Chihuahua Boy was a sidekick for Kyle, but Jed's sidekicks weren't as visible. I'm sure someone put him up to it in the first place; they probably even dared him to beat me up. To look cool to his friends, he took the dare and started the fight. Deep down, I don't think he really wanted to fight me, but negative peer pressure swayed him. Jed is easy to understand and easy to forgive, and I do forgive him.

Then there was Kyle with his sidekick Chihuahua Boy, and Nick the upperclassman I met on the ecology/nature field trip. Kyle and Nick, along with the many other nameless faces who felt the need to fight me, call me names, or in some other way ridicule or demean me, can all be categorized as guys who were trying to find themselves and find friends by acting tough and "cool" (at least what they defined as cool). I was an easy target, a guaranteed win. I was chosen because they were afraid of losing a fight. Fear, jealously, and a desire to fit in with a group—any group—drove them to do what they did. These bullies are a little more difficult to forgive, because they never showed any remorse. Still, their actions were motivated out of their own insecurities, shortcomings, and fears, not because they were inherently or consistently heartless and mean.

You've probably heard a lot about peer pressure, both good and bad. Jed, Kyle, Nick, and others were living examples of the ugly side of peer pressure. Their desire to be noticed and to look cool or tough drove them to pick fights with me or ridicule me. Although there's no excuse for what they did, I can forgive them because they were really just trying to find their own identity or lash out in response to something else that was going on in their lives. Unfortunately, they chose a poor way of dealing with the teenage turmoil they were feeling. I understand that, and I can forgive them now, although it has taken quite a few years to feel forgiving toward them.

After trying to understand a bully's real motivations, the next most important thing to understand is that it isn't your fault (unless, of course, you started the bullying in the first place). Usually a bully is going through the same kind of teen and preteen difficulties that you are—maybe even worse. It doesn't justify their actions, but it helps to know that it isn't your fault.

When it comes to bullies, it's not you, it's them.

What about Sheri? Can I forgive her for being the trigger of my depression? Can I forgive her for treating me like an escapee from a leper colony just because I asked her out on a date? During my high school years, I couldn't. It's true that her actions were the proverbial straw that broke the camel's back. They weren't the only cause of my fragile self-esteem, but that piece of straw on my back felt more like a tree stump.

For a long time, I blamed Sheri for launching me into several years of dark, and sometimes frightening, feelings of self-loathing and worthlessness. Despite that, I can forgive her now. Completely. How? It started with perspective and understanding.

First, perspective. I realize now that the trigger for my depression could have been anything: an embarrassing moment; a harsh, personal criticism from someone I admired; a poor grade in one of my best courses; or a rejection from any girl I considered a friend. In short, my depression was already armed and primed. Almost any spark might have set it off, even one that was less severe than the cold rejection from Sheri.

Second, understanding. That cold, frosty night when I asked Sheri out on a date, I caught her off guard. Peer pressure didn't have anything to do with it because there wasn't anyone else around and no one was there to overhear. When caught off guard, most people react in a defensive manner to protect themselves from potential hurt, embarrassment, or even just emotional awkwardness. That's what she did. It was a knee-jerk reaction to lie to avoid an awkward situation. The problem was, she had to face up to that lie the following Monday, but she couldn't, so she avoided me like the plague.

Perhaps more important than being caught off guard, I believe Sheri was unprepared. That may sound like the same thing, but being caught off guard or surprised is different from being unprepared. You can be prepared for something, yet still be surprised when it happens (see the Rejection sidebar in this chapter).

Now to Vince, the locker room bully, how can I forgive him? This is a really tough one for me, but I know I need to do it, for my own healing if nothing else. Even understanding him is difficult, if not impossible. Because understanding is the beginning of forgiveness, I'll start there.

Vince never showed the slightest trace of remorse. He even raised his voice when ridiculing me so that everyone nearby could hear him. I didn't catch him off guard, either; he repeatedly went looking for me to pour out his brand of insult. He enjoyed being a bully and tried his best to humiliate me. I think he was proud of his behavior rather than ashamed of it.

How can I understand Vince and his actions? Well, it's quite possible Vince was jealous of me, although I'm sure he would never admit it. I had good grades, I was smart, and I didn't get into trouble. He was the opposite. Despite his success in sports, he was only a mediocre student.

Then again, maybe who I was didn't matter to him. Maybe he was just so full of himself that he really did look down on people he thought were weaklings or sports challenged like I was. Or maybe he was just a jerk, rotten to the core, and he was only being himself.

I'm not getting very far on the understanding part, am I? Let's try another tack. Vince was short and got mediocre grades so maybe without realizing it he was trying to make up for that with bullying and bravados. Maybe, contrary to outward appearances, his self-esteem

Rejection

How can you be prepared to reject someone who asks you out on a date? For some reason, we don't teach our children how to reject someone sensitively and kindly, yet clearly. Most boys and girls, even men and women, are terrible at rejecting someone who asks them out on a date or shows interest in them. Lies, avoidance, and downright meanness seem to be the natural patterns that people fall into when rejecting someone, but we often fail to consider the emotional consequences they reap on the recipient.

If you have ever experienced rejection, think about the people who rejected you harshly and hurtfully. Did you catch him or her off guard? Did he or she react with lies or meanness? Is it possible he or she had never learned a better way to respond? When it comes to personal relationships, most of us make it up as we go. Imagine building a house with no training: It would be a sloppy, rickety, haphazard building that you would probably not want to live in, much less enjoy looking at. Most interpersonal situations, especially when we're first learning how to interact with the opposite sex, are just like that: sloppy, rickety, and haphazard.

Besides not being taught how to reject someone with sensitivity and caring, rejecting someone can give the rejector a cruel sense of power and control. This brings out the mean, uncaring emotions that lie within each of us. The only way to avoid letting yourself fall into the trap of rejecting people harshly, insensitively, and cruelly is to think about how you want to do it ahead of time. In other words, be prepared. Practice how you might reject someone in a kind way so that when you are caught off guard your first reaction will be to recite one of your well-rehearsed, carefully thought-out lines, rather than relying on a gut instinct of cruelty, avoidance, or lies.

You might be saying to yourself, "Why should I bother? He's scummy or weird or a geek, so why should I care about his feelings anyway?" Whether you call it following the Golden Rule, avoiding "burning bridges," or just being considerate, being aware of and sensitive to the feelings of others is a good personality trait to have and one that will serve you well throughout your life. That doesn't mean you have to like everyone, but you should treat people with dignity and sensitivity, whether you like them or not.

wasn't all that high either, but he covered it up with obnoxious behavior. Some people do that.

I suppose it's possible he identified a little too closely with his sports teammates, considering everyone outside his clique to be inferior. Maybe his parents never taught him to treat other people with respect, so he was just relying on base animal instincts of aggression and cruelty. I really don't know which, if any, of these reasons is the right one. Maybe all of them made Vince act the way he did.

Although understanding Vince is very difficult, I can at least imagine several plausible reasons for his behavior, some of which fall into that category of "struggling with personal identity" that so many teens have experienced, including myself. If I can at least partially understand him, can I forgive him? That's still difficult.

Why have I avoided forgiving him so far? Sometimes I think we resist forgiving people because denying forgiveness makes us feel as though we're hurting them back, getting them back for what they did to us. We feel as though we have extracted our revenge or at least not let them "off the hook." A denial of forgiveness, however, is an action that exists only in our minds. We're the only ones who feel anything, good or bad. A revengeful denial of forgiveness is probably part of what has kept me from forgiving Vince all these years, but no healing can be found in revenge, so I know I have to overcome that desire.

Another way we deal with emotional hurt is to pass judgment, deciding who deserves our forgiveness and who does not based on our own personal opinion of their worthiness to receive it. I know I have done that. If you forgive only people you like, however, it's not a very genuine form of forgiveness.

If I've withheld forgiveness to be hurtful and judgmental, then I start to wonder if maybe, in a way, I'm no better than some of the bullies who hurt me. I just bottled it up inside, whereas they acted it out physically or verbally. Perhaps that's the twisting path to forgiveness—looking at ourselves first to see how our *own* actions might have been hurtful to others.

I remember one such incident in middle school when my actions were hurtful to someone else. I was riding the bus to school that day.

The bus driver had stopped to pick up a girl a year or two younger than I was. She always seemed a bit strange. She was short and had messy blonde hair in a bowl-shaped cut. She wore big, thick "Coke-bottle" glasses, and she always sat shyly by herself on the bus, never talking to anyone. A couple of the other kids were starting to tease her that day, and for some reason, which is beyond me, I started joining in, teasing her about her silly looking hair, her thick glasses, and how strange she was. I don't remember exactly what I said, but I know it must have hurt.

I can't believe I did that! Of *all* people, I should have known better. She was very much like me, more so than I would have liked to admit at that age. I'd felt that shyness before. I'd felt the pain of that kind of teasing before, and I'd felt the fear of the bullies on the bus. Yet, like a lemming rushing to the sea, I joined in with the others to hurl ridicules at her. The teasing didn't last long, but it didn't matter; a few viciously chosen words can do a lifetime of damage.

I feel terrible about that incident. Even to this day, I cringe whenever I think about it, and I've never forgiven myself for it. My actions that morning on the school bus were worse than any of the bullies I had experienced, because I *knew* first hand the pain I was causing, but I didn't stop myself.

Did I ever apologize to that little girl on the bus? I don't remember. If I was a typical teenager, I probably didn't, even if I had thought about it. I wonder now, does she feel as angry with me and unforgiving of me today as I am of Vince? Does Vince feel the same awful, painful guilt about his actions as I do for the ridicule I gave that girl? If I desperately want to forgive myself for what I did to her, how can I deny Vince the forgiveness he may need for what he did?

We all make the same mistakes, one way or another. We hurt each other out of our own selfish need for recognition or attention. We ridicule people so we can, for a brief moment, feel better about ourselves or feel powerful. We take cheap shots at people, attempting to build ourselves up by knocking others down. It's cruel and it's wrong.

To that little blonde-haired girl on the bus, I apologize. I'm sorry for not treating you with the same kind of respect with which I wanted to be treated. I should have known better. Please forgive me. And Vince, I forgive you. From the bottom of my heart, Vince, I forgive you.

Your Thoughts

+ Think of someone you've been mean to or bullied in the past. Write a letter of apology. If you think you can bring yourself do it, send the letter to him or her or apologize in person. If not, keep the letter to remind yourself of changes you want to make in the way you treat other people.

+ As you read this chapter, did you start your own journey of forgiveness? If you haven't already done so, take out a piece of paper and jot down some notes about the people you need to forgive. Start by writing down ways that you can understand them or their behavior and then move on to why you can forgive them.

+ How do you deal with the anger you feel when someone hurts you? Do you bottle it up inside, letting it painfully fester and grow as I did? Do you lash out with your anger, hurting other people as a result? What is the best way to deal with that anger?

Group Discussion

+ Forgiveness sometimes seems like a forgotten topic, especially when we watch the evening news and hear about road rage, revenge killings or students going on a shooting rampage at their school. Is this kind of violence common, or is the media reporting on only the most sensational news they can find? Do you think there is a critical lack of forgiveness and understanding in your community, your country, or the world? Why?

✦ In what ways does society either support or discourage forgiveness? Do we glorify the rage of revenge in movies and video games, or is that just harmless entertainment?

✦ When someone tells us he or she is sorry for hurting our feelings, do we always graciously accept the apology, or do we sometimes use it as an opportunity to viciously tell the person off, attempting to hurt him or her right back?

✦ Group exercise: Role-play dating rejection. Pick people to role-play asking someone out on a date and getting a rejection. Have the group make suggestions to both the rejector and the rejected for ways to ask someone on a date in a polite, respectful, and not pushy way and how to reject someone clearly but with sensitivity and kindness. Discuss the pros and cons of different approaches to each.

11

Forgiveness and Understanding: Your Parents and Yourself

If you haven't forgiven yourself something,
how can you forgive others?

—DOLORES HUERTA

Why does it hurt so much and for so long when a parent makes an insensitive or hurtful comment to us? How can the people who are supposed to love you the most be so hurtful? A harsh or uncaring remark from a parent can injure more deeply and broadly than any bully's actions. Why?

Maybe it hurts so much because we expect our parents to be "Mr. and Mrs. Totally Perfect"—always caring, thoughtful, generous, patient, and understanding. I noticed that when my children were young, they looked up to my wife and me with a glowing, unconditional admiration and love. Perhaps that unrealistic, yet wonderful, perception of our parents stays with us in the back of our minds, raising our expectations of them long after we've realized they aren't without their own faults and hang-ups.

Maybe it's also because of our nearly complete reliance on our parents for our self-respect and self-esteem, particularly at a young age. It is both a blessing and at times a curse that we are so dependent on them in this way. This reliance can be both a great source of strength and a source of weakness. This reliance and dependence makes a hurtful comment ten times more painful coming from a parent than someone our own age.

The fact that we live with our parents can make the hurt last longer. We can't just walk away from them or completely avoid them in the same way we might avoid someone at school, at least not very easily. Even physically walking away from your parents for a short time doesn't change the fact that they are your parents and that they will be your parents for the rest of your life, affecting and guiding you in both good and bad ways even long after they've passed away.

Perhaps it is all these reasons, tangled up in the complex web of a parent–teen relationship, that makes a hurtful comment from them so painful and long lasting. I doubt we can ever entirely untangle this web, but you can be certain that the complex relationship you have with your parents *will* change as you get older, especially after high school.

Your parents are human and always will be. So are you. Forgive them and forgive yourself. You deserve it and so do your parents. Forgiveness and understanding will go a long way toward helping you survive your teen and preteen years.

The incident with my dad and my nearly straight-A report card was one of those long-lasting, painful moments for me. Twenty years later, it still stings when I think about it and replay it in my mind. I can still feel the sense of letdown and anger, the rage of wanting to shred my report card into a thousand pieces after he dismissed it so casually and carelessly. The years have only slightly diminished the strength of the memory even though, as you'll see later in this chapter, I understand the incident and my dad better now and I'm no longer angry about it.

More than years, though, having children of my own has shed new light on the subject for me. Being a parent has made it extremely obvious to me how imperfect and human we all are as parents. Try as I might to be the perfect dad, I am no closer to perfect than my parents were to me. With my own parenting, I might have improved or corrected some of their mistakes—the ones that lay branded in my memory—but I have committed my own mistakes, some small and some that were whoppers.

You know how parents sometimes get so mad at you that they say mean, hurtful things to you? Been there, done that, wished I hadn't. Do you hate it when your mom or dad threatens to take a garbage bag and throw your things away if you don't clean your room? Yeah, I've done that, too. Have you had an experience like my report card day, when your parents are too wrapped up in their own problems and worries to acknowledge you and your accomplishments? I did that to my own son not long ago. I should have recognized the similarity to my own report card day incident with my dad, but I didn't see the resemblance until it was too late. I hope he doesn't resent it as I did for many years. I hope he can forgive me.

No matter how hard we try, no matter how calm we try to keep ourselves, parents lose it sometimes. We lose our self-control, we lose our patience, and sometimes we lose that filter in our head that keeps mean things from coming out of our mouths. Has that ever happened to you when dealing with a parent, brother or sister, or even a friend? Chances are it has. I'm not making excuses for this very human behavior, nor am I trying to justify it; I'm saying that's the way people are from time to time.

© Zits Partnership, King Features Syndicate. Reprinted with permission.

Just because parents make occasional mistakes, that doesn't excuse a repeated pattern of verbal or physical abuse. Abusive behavior requires professional counseling for both you and your parents. What I'm talking about in this chapter are the kind of mistakes parents make simply because they are human beings who can't be 100 percent perfect 100 percent of the time. Even the best parents can make mistakes that hurt you deeply. Accidentally hurting people we love is probably as old a behavior as the human race itself.

Your parents are human. They're not perfect and never will be. Anger and frustration will cloud their judgment and shorten their tempers. They will make mistakes. Some will be little, some will be incredibly huge, some will be easy to brush off, and others will sting for years. It's the nature of human beings. I can guarantee that you will also make mistakes as a parent someday. We all do.

Forgiving and understanding your parents begins with the knowledge that they are not perfect and they cannot be perfect because they are human. Maybe we can fault our parents for not trying as hard they could or not being as understanding or loving as we would like them to be, but we can't fault them for being human. They are subject to the same pain, stress, anxiety, worries, and fears that every other person in the world—including you—are subject to.

Pain, anxiety, worry, fear, and stress all affect your parent's ability to give you the understanding, caring, and love that you so desperately need from them. Just as your emotions can go up and down on a daily or hourly basis, so can theirs. It's impossible to always be a sensitive, caring parent who always says the right things at the right time, never saying an unkind or hurtful word.

Now that I'm an adult and a parent, I can easily imagine the events and emotions that led up to the report card incident with my father. I know he was unhappy with his job and he probably had a miserable, unfulfilling, and stressful day at work. He left work for the day and came home to the stress of parenting two teenagers, worrying about money and being anxious about the sometimes overwhelming number of responsibilities of being an adult and parent. He came home to a son he didn't really understand, a son who was in some ways very similar to him but in other ways completely different.

Communicating with Your Parents

When you talk with your parents, does it seem like you're talking to someone from another world? Communicating with your parents can be frustrating and stressful (and it can be for them, too) because we have different backgrounds, experiences, and, most important, different perspectives. How can you make communicating less painful and get your parents to listen to you more?

+ Avoid whining, yelling, or using a nasty tone of voice. Nothing will make a parent stop listening to you faster than those three approaches to communicating. It's human nature to resort to whining, yelling, or nastiness when you're feeling angry, but these will kill any progress you hope to make with your parents.
+ Be clear and direct. Your parents can't read your mind any better than you can read theirs. If you want something, need something, or just want them to hear you, speak clearly and directly to your point.
+ Use a mature tone and style. Your parents are accustomed to speaking with adults, so they are more likely to listen to you if you talk to them like an adult, using a calm, mature, and well-thought-out way of speaking. If you use this technique, they will probably be so impressed that they will be "all ears."
+ Take a time out if the discussion gets too heated. If you feel that you're losing control of yourself or your emotions while talking with your parents, ask to take a break for five, ten, or fifteen minutes to calm down (pick a calming and comforting place such as your bedroom). It's best to agree on the "take a break" technique before the discussion starts, because once it gets heated up it's difficult for everyone to stop. We use this technique in our family. If anyone—teenager or parent—feels that he or she is "losing it," we ask to take a break and restart the discussion in a few minutes. It was difficult to do this at first, but now we all recognize the benefits of cooling down the discussion.

I can imagine how he dwelled on these emotions on his way home from work that day, letting the negative feelings feed on themselves in a vicious cycle, growing more angry, frustrated, and dissatisfied by the minute. All he wanted to do was unwind and forget his troubles by watching TV. Then I bounded down the stairs all cheerful and excited, interrupting his relaxation and expecting a warm, loving welcome and a hearty pat on the back for a job well done.

It didn't happen. How could it?

You might say he should have known better anyway, that he should have put his feelings aside and been supportive of me anyway (and you have probably felt that way about your parents at one point or another in your life). Maybe he should have, but what we should do and what we're emotionally able to do at a given moment in time are sometimes two different things.

© Zits Partnership, King Features Syndicate. Reprinted with permission.

I now know how difficult it can be to remain calm and collected, sensitive, and caring toward your children when you're feeling frustrated and disgruntled about your work, your financial situation, your marriage, your parenting ability, your children's behavior or any number of other weights that life can bear down on you as an adult. As hard as I try to put those concerns aside when dealing with my own children, sometimes I just can't do it; I lose my temper and I make a mistake that I regret later.

If you're fortunate, your parents realize their mistakes and are willing to apologize for them. Some can, others cannot. Some parents may realize their mistakes, but they are afraid or unwilling to apologize for fear it will undermine their parental authority over their children.

Even when a parent wants to apologize, it can be particularly difficult to apologize to your own children. A parent has to cut himself or herself down a few notches to be able to apologize. It's far easier to apologize to someone you consider an equal; it is far harder to apologize to someone over whom you believe you have authority.

If your parents don't apologize for their mistakes, look for other outward signs of regret and remorse such as a kind word, a pat on the back, or a smile directed at you at some point after they've calmed down and thought about their actions. Take those signs to heart, just like an apology. Sometimes that's the best a parent can do.

If you're a parent reading this book, I'm not suggesting you don't have a responsibility to apologize. There's no substitute for a heartfelt, face-to-face apology; it can do wonders for your child's self-esteem. However, if you can't bring yourself to do that, find some way to let your child know that you still love and care for him or her. Ask yourself, is it more important for me to save face and assert my authority, or is it more important to undo the harm I might have done to my son or daughter?

If you're a teen or preteen reading this book, remember that forgiveness and understanding goes both ways. It's as much your responsibility to try to apologize, as it is your parents. If you show a willingness to apologize and be forgiving, maybe that will help break down the emotional barriers that are preventing your parents from doing the same. The same goes for conflicts with your friends, too. An act of kindness and forgiveness on your part may be just the reassurance your friend needs to feel forgiving as well.

Now, how about forgiving yourself? Have you ever made mistakes for which you were angry and unforgiving of yourself? I know I did, plenty of times. I would beat myself up emotionally for almost any mistake. We all do it at some point in our lives. It's in our nature.

We can be particularly hard on ourselves during the teenage years for things such as getting poor grades, failing tryouts for a sports team, doing poorly on a test, or getting rejected by a girl or boy we desperately want to date. It's far too easy to blame ourselves for every bad thing that happens to us. We beat ourselves up over our shortcomings and our apparent lack of talent, ability, or good looks.

You need to forgive yourself, too. You're human. You're not a superhuman who can be talented at everything. Most of us are only talented or successful at one or two things. When it comes to grades or sports, you can only ask yourself, "Did I give it my best? Did I apply myself to the best of my ability, or did I just give it a half-hearted effort?" You can only get angry with yourself if you didn't give it your all.

When it comes to rejection by a boy or girl you wanted to like you, all you can do is move on and realize that it probably wasn't meant to be. It's not that fate has anything to do with it; if the emotional and physical chemistry doesn't go equally both ways, then a relationship wasn't meant to be and never could be. In that case, you're better off looking elsewhere until you find someone who likes you and wants to be with you as much as you like and want to be with him or her.

Forgiveness and understanding are tough. If they were easy, everyone would practice them all the time. You've probably heard the maxim "nothing worth doing is easy." It's difficult to think of a better example of that than forgiveness and understanding.

Your Thoughts

+ Think about something one or both of your parents said to you that really hurt. Think about the situation that surrounded that incident. What stresses or frustrations were your parents experiencing at the time that might have contributed to them being hurtful? Were they facing job layoffs, financial trouble, or marital trouble? Could they have just had a bad day at work? Can you forgive them? Why or why not?

+ Think of a situation in which you were really hard on yourself for a goal you didn't achieve: a poor grade on a test or a competition you lost. Do you still want to achieve the goal or win the competition? Then make a list of concrete and realistic steps to achieve that goal. Don't just keep the list in your head; write it down on paper. The act of writing them down commits goals to memory more effectively than just keeping them in your head. After you write your goals down, put your list in a noticeable place so you will see it often. Also, remember to forgive yourself so you can move on and learn from the experience.

Group Discussion

✦ Blaming our parents for our problems is common—we all like to do it. But how many of our problems are really our parent's fault and how many are no one's fault but our own? Give examples and discuss.

✦ What kinds of parental mistakes or behaviors can have a truly damaging effect on a teen or preteen? How might you deal with these mistakes?

✦ How can you set reasonable yet challenging expectations for yourself (not just now, but at any time of your life)? How can you strive to excel and succeed, yet accept failure when it happens? How should you *define* success and failure?

✦ Do some people avoid doing anything challenging because they fear they might fail? If you know someone like that, what words of advice could you offer to help him or her forge ahead despite the fear of failure?

✦ Is forgiving your parents or yourself a sign of weakness, or is it a sign of strength?

✦ If your parents don't apologize for their mistakes, and they don't show any sign of remorse or regret, should you forgive them anyway? Why or why not?

12

Perspective

I find that it is not the circumstances in which we are placed,
but the spirit in which we face them, that constitutes our comfort.

—ELIZABETH T. KING

"Oh, things aren't that bad, are they? They could be worse, right?"

Whenever I heard friends say something like that, I knew they were right; I needed to put things in perspective. At the same time, I was irritated because I thought they were trivializing my problems or brushing them off. The conflicts you feel as a teen or preteen are very real, no matter how big or small. Whether it's a rejection from the "girl or boy of your dreams," being the victim of bullying and teasing, or just feeling out of place and unnoticed, your feelings are real and at times intense. Emotional pain and anguish are just as real as any physical pain. A good perspective, though, can reduce the pain or anguish to more manageable levels.

Why is it so difficult to put our problems in perspective during our adolescent years? I believe at that age, you just don't have many years of life experience on which to build a perspective. When you're down on yourself because you're not popular or you don't fit in, it's difficult to believe it's going to be any other way because you've never *known* any other way. You don't have the years of experience to believe your life will change.

I have to admit I wasn't very good at putting my problems in perspective during my teen years. Every failure, rejection, or embarrassing moment seemed traumatic and devastating at the time. I took myself and my problems far too seriously. Sometimes I put problems into perspective, and that did help, but most of the time it was too difficult for me to do.

Let's take a look at my life as a teen from the perspective I now have as an adult with more years of experience behind me. Did I wallow in self-pity too much? Yes, I did. Was I oversensitive? Yes, I was. Was I too hard on myself, especially when I was rejected by a girl? Definitely. Was I at times foolish and gullible? Yes. Was that all part of growing up and maturing? Absolutely!

That's great, you might be saying, but what about *my* life? How can I put my life in perspective *now,* instead of waiting until I'm an adult? In this chapter, I present five paths to perspective. These paths are five ways of looking at your life that can help you put your problems in perspective and make them more manageable. Although your negative and painful feelings are real and legitimate, you really do have tremendous power to control how those feelings affect you.

Perspective can smooth out the roller-coaster ride. It can give you hope for your future and strength to persevere. Perspective is power.

Perspective Is Power—Five Paths to Perspective

1. When it comes to bullies, they have a problem, not you.
2. You aren't the only person going through what you are going through.
3. You're not done baking yet.
4. Seven years is a short time.
5. If you look at yourself and your life from a distance, you'll gain a better perspective.

Path 1: When It Comes to Bullies, They Have a Problem, Not You

Bullies are thieves. They are so desperate for a sense of power or importance that they need to rob someone else of their happiness to get it. The problem is, unlike thieves, there are no doors with locks to keep them out of your life. You have to face them every day in school. Although there are no locks, there is perspective, and maybe that's a more powerful tool. If we can learn to deal with bullying, name calling, and teasing now, we'll be that much stronger to face other challenges in our lives in the future.

Bullies are often cowardly sheep in wolves' clothing. Although some are strong and powerful on both the inside and outside, others, like Jed, are truly weak and afraid on the inside. They use bullying as a way to cover up that weakness so no one can see the frightened child within.

Often bullies have been bullied themselves, causing them to throw their pain and anger at other people in retaliation. These bullies use their behavior as an attempt to rebuild their self-esteem and self-concept or to "get back at the world" for what has been done to them.

Whenever someone calls you names, teases you, or bullies you, remind yourself, "It's not me, it's them." They are so desperate to feel good that they have to steal happiness from you. They can't find their own happiness, so they take it from others. They have a problem, not you, so don't blame yourself for their behavior.

I don't want to paint a picture that all bullies are inherently bad people. Sometimes even the nicest, most decent people can be pressured or dared into bullying behavior, and even the most decent person can slide into selfishness at some point in his or her life. It's human nature to want to feel good about ourselves, and sometimes we choose immature and hurtful ways of achieving that feeling.

Even people who regularly bully others may not realize the pain they are inflicting on their victims. They might be too absorbed in their own problems or too thrilled with the false sense of power that bullying can provide to stop and think about the pain they may be causing. That doesn't justify bullying behavior, but knowing that some bullies are motivated more by selfishness than an actual intent to cause hurt can take a little of the sting out of their actions.

Put bullies into perspective. Remember that their own personal struggles may be the cause of their bullying. Instead of hating them, try feeling sorry for them, or at the very least ignore or brush-off their attempts to hurt you. However you deal with them, don't keep their behavior a secret. You need to tell a parent, counselor, or teacher about their behavior, not just to help yourself, but to prevent what is happening to you from happening to other people, too.

Group Exercise—Name-Calling

Have you ever heard someone say (or yourself thought) something like this: "She's so overly sensitive. I mean, really, so someone called her a name. Big deal. She should just get over it." Discuss this statement in your group.

After the discussion, give each person a piece of paper and have each person write a hurtful or mean word or phrase on it. Be realistic. Choose words or phrases you have heard, have thought of saying, or might hear at your school.

When everyone has finished writing, sit on the floor in a circle and have one person say his or her mean word or phrase out loud then put the piece of paper, writing side up, in the center of the circle. Ask a few people at random how they feel about it. Has it affected them in any way?

Now have the other people in the group say their words or phrases out loud one at a time then place their pieces of paper in the center of the circle. When everyone is finished, once again ask a few people at random how they feel. Has there been a change in the responses? If so, discuss why.

Consider a person who might receive these hurtful words or phrases from not only one person at a time, but from four, five, or maybe ten people each day, day after day, month after month. Now read the quote at the beginning of this sidebar. Discuss how it makes you feel.

Path 2: You Aren't the Only Person Going Through What You Are Going Through

If there's one perspective that's easy to understand and believe, it's that you're not the only person going through tough times. When you walk in the hallways at school, look at the faces of your classmates and listen to what you hear in passing. What emotions do you see or hear? Many people cover up their emotions, but others wear them on their faces or in their words. If you look closely and listen carefully, you'll see other people who are struggling too. Often their struggles are the same as yours.

Most teens and preteens feel bad about themselves at some time. It might be because they failed a test, were rejected by a crush, or just don't feel like they fit in. Believe it or not, almost everyone feels that way at some time. If you do, there's nothing wrong with you. In fact, if you feel that way on occasion, you're quite normal.

© Zits Partnership, King Features Syndicate. Reprinted with permission.

Remember Jed, the bully from my first fight? Jed, "Mr. Tough Guy," was crying in the principal's office. He was going through something. When I started wondering what his problems might be, I couldn't help but feel a little compassion for him. It softened me and took some of the sting out of my anger and resentment. Maybe he wasn't struggling with the exact same issues that I was, but his struggle was very real just the same. It helped to know that in some way we were both "in the same boat."

Whenever you're bullied, called names, or rejected by someone in a cruel, harsh manner, consider what problems that person might be going through as well. It doesn't take much thought to realize that their problems are very real and sometimes even transparently clear.

Having the perspective that you're not alone in your struggles isn't just helpful in dealing with bullies and name calling. By realizing that most teens are going through the same conflicts and by inference assuming that most adults today went through the same conflicts, you can know and believe that these problems are typical and they won't last forever. You *can* persevere and overcome them, survive, and even thrive into adulthood. Millions of people have done it before, and so can you!

Path 3: You're Not Done Baking Yet

This may sound like a funny analogy, but it is an apt and memorable one: You are like cookies baking in an oven. You're still growing and taking shape. You're still maturing, learning, and developing. You're starting to look like the finished product, but you're not done baking yet.

Remember, you didn't learn to ride a bike or swim or roller skate the first time you did it, right? It took trial and error and a lot of patience and persistence to make it happen. Life is like that too. Learning takes time, patience, and persistence. Relationships take time, patience, and persistence. Almost everything good in life takes trial and error, patience, and persistence. You will be learning about life, relationships, and yourself for the rest of your life, so don't expect yourself to have it all figured out right now.

The natural conclusion to draw from the baking cookie perspective is this: go easy on yourself. Don't expect yourself to be perfect at sports, perfect at dating, perfect at music, or perfect at taking tests. As you learn, you'll change. As you grow and mature, you will change. You're still learning and developing. Always try your best at everything you do, of course, but remember you're not done baking yet.

Here's a challenge for you: Whenever you say you can't do something or something doesn't seem right in your life, try adding the word "yet."

"No one wants to date me . . . yet."

"No one likes me . . . yet."

"I'm not good at sports . . . yet."

"I don't know what I want to do with my life . . . yet."

"I don't like myself . . . yet."

For much of my teen and preteen years, I said and believed each of these statements about myself, but I didn't add "yet." I thought

The Teenage Brain

The idea that "you're not done baking yet" is more than just a useful perspective: It is a reality of the adolescent brain. Recent brain research using magnetic resonance imaging (MRI) technology has revealed the following:

✦ The human brain undergoes a major growth of new brain cells just before puberty.

✦ Our brains "prune" and manage these new brain cells as we learn and grow.

✦ During adolescence, certain brain activities move from a part of the brain called the superior temporal sulcus, near the rear of the brain, to the medial prefrontal cortex, near the front of the brain. This front region of the brain is responsible for higher level thinking, such as thinking about the consequences of your actions in terms of other peoples' emotions and feelings.

✦ Our brains don't finish their development until the age of twenty to thirty, well beyond what we normally consider the growing up years.

Sources

National Institute of Mental Health
http://www.nimh.nih.gov/Publicat/teenbrain.cfm

BBC News
http://news.bbc.co.uk

things would always be the way they were then. I was wrong. All the negative things I believed about myself turned out to be wrong once I reached adulthood. For example, I'm still not great at sports, but I'm better than I ever was during my teenage years.

Get a piece of paper or your journal and write "yet" sentences for yourself based on your own experiences. Use my "yet" sentences above or the examples below to help you brainstorm your own:

> "I just don't get math . . . yet."
> "I can't make a basket in basketball . . . yet."
> "I don't have any friends or even know how to make friends . . . yet."
> "I didn't make the track team . . . yet."
> "I'm not good at anything . . . yet."
> "There's nothing special about me . . . yet."

Don't believe that the way you feel now as a teen or preteen is the way you'll always feel for the rest of your life. Remember, you're not done baking yet.

Path 4: Seven Years Is a Short Time

"Are you kidding?" you're probably saying. I know, seven years feels like an eternity when you're growing up. Even the time from one birthday to the next seems to take forever. Sometimes you think you'll never become an adult.

Let's put seven years in perspective with a short exercise. Get some blank paper, scissors, a marker, and some tape, then follow these instructions:

1. Cut the paper into strips about one inch wide.
2. Tape the strips together to make one long strip at least forty inches long.
3. Now draw a line across the strip every half inch over the length of the strip. When you are done, you should have

roughly eighty lines drawn. Your strip should resemble a long ladder.

4. Start counting lines at one end of the strip; with your marker, color in the area from line eleven through line eighteen. These represent your teen and preteen years.

Now that you've made your strip, lay it down on the floor and stand above it. Look how small the seven years are when compared with your entire potential lifeline of eighty years (assuming good health, that's a reasonable life expectancy). Those seven years are really short, aren't they? They can seem like an entire lifetime given how slowly they pass, but when compared with the rest of your life, they are really short.

Now look at the rest of the lines, the ones past the years colored with marker. That's the rest of your life. Those are the years of your true and best life. Not all those years will go well, and not all of them will live up to your expectations, but many of them will. Overall, the quality of your adult life will probably exceed your current expectations. The years *after* age eighteen or nineteen are typically the best years of your life. Those years are a gift to use as you choose.

Keep your lifeline strip in a safe place where you'll remember it. As major events or milestones occur in your life, write them down on that strip of paper. When you have a significant success or achievement, write it down. When you look back on your lifeline years later, you'll almost certainly see that your best years were the years *after* age eighteen or nineteen.

Do whatever it takes to get through the tough times you might be experiencing now so you can discover the gift of your true life waiting for you in adulthood.

Path 5: If You Look at Yourself and Your Life from a Distance, You'll Gain a Better Perspective

Sometimes we wallow in our own misery and self-pity so much that we can't see the good things around us in our lives. Trust me, I know. During my teen years, I think I elevated wallowing in self-pity to an art form.

The best perspective can sometimes be from a distance. If you look at your life too closely—cross-examining and torturing yourself for every failure, mishap, and embarrassing moment—you can't see beyond to the positive things that may be happening all around you, even things you desperately want to see. Apollo 16 astronaut Thomas K. Mattingly II once said, "It's very hard to take yourself too seriously when you look at the world from outer space." The same is true for life in general. Taking a mental look at yourself from a distance can really help put things in perspective.

Do you remember my band trip to Florida and the embarrassing, silent rejection I received from Jenna? As you can imagine, it was a very long bus trip back to Wisconsin, both in miles and self-imposed misery. I must have replayed the incident with Jenna dozens of times in my mind on the bus ride back home. Sometimes I would replay it to imagine what I might have done differently. Could I have seen Paul's deception if I hadn't been so eager for Jenna to like me? Could I have said something different to her, something that would have made her like me more, something that would have at least generated a response?

Other times I would replay the scene in my mind purely for the sake of self-torture, reminding myself with every replay of how worthless and undesirable I was. After all, Jenna was so disgusted at the thought of dancing with me, or even talking with me, that she was speechless.

Somewhere in the midst of my self-pity and torture on the bus ride home, another girl in the band, who I'll call Sandra, walked down the bus aisle to retrieve a bag from one of the overhead bins directly above my seat on the bus. She put a hand on my shoulder for support as she reached up high. After retrieving the item, she smiled and returned to the back of the bus. I thought nothing of it at the time, but it stayed in my memory for some reason.

It wasn't until several years later that I remembered that moment on the bus and rethought Sandra's actions. I remember her hand lingering on my shoulder far longer than necessary to retrieve the bag.

Her smile said much more than just "pardon me"; she made direct eye contact and gave me a warm and inviting smile. She had made a pass at me! Her message was as clear as a bell, without a word spoken, yet I hadn't noticed her because I was too busy wallowing in my self-pity, too busy convincing myself that no girl would ever like me or would ever want to go on a date with me.

While I was wallowing, I didn't notice, right in front of me, the very thing I was so desperately seeking: someone to like me for who I was, someone who was attracted to *me*. I was blinded by my own self-pity.

It's easy to dwell on the negative. In some strange, weird way, it can even feel good to wallow in our own negative thoughts. But when we dwell on the negative, we can't see the positive, even if it's right in front of us.

Take a look around and see both the world and people close to you more objectively. If you're looking at yourself too closely, you're not looking around you. Ask yourself, "Am I really as unattractive and untalented as I think I am? Is it possible that my feeling of loneliness is temporary? Is it possible that someday, the people or events that bring me down now won't matter to me anymore or at least won't hurt as much? Is it possible there is someone out there who really likes me, but I have been too self-absorbed to notice?"

Remember to take a step back to look at yourself from a distance. The new perspective can be refreshing and illuminating. And the roller coaster doesn't look so big from far away.

Your Thoughts

+ Of the paths presented in this chapter, which do you believe will help you the most? Do you have your own paths that help you even more?
+ How can you remember and apply the most helpful paths to your life? Make a plan for how you will apply perspective to your life. Write down your plan in a

journal or diary or write your favorite perspective statements on a piece of paper and tape it to the back of your bedroom door. Whatever you do, plan a way that will frequently remind you of the perspectives that will help the most.

Group Discussion

✦ Why do some people have an easier time putting things into perspective than others? Is it just their personality or a mixture of personality, training, upbringing and life experiences? Can someone learn to put things in perspective?

✦ Do you think sensitive people are less mature than their peers or is sensitivity just part of their personality? Do you think being sensitive is a good thing or a bad thing? Why?

✦ When does sensitivity become oversensitivity? Who defines that boundary and why?

✦ If you have a friend who is having a tough time putting life's problems in perspective, how might you help him or her without seeming to pry or without offending your friend? Think of a way that doesn't involve platitudes such as "Don't worry so much," or "Your problems aren't so bad." No one appreciates having his or her feelings minimized or dismissed.

13
Faith

*There is no merit where there is no trial; and till experience stamps
the mark of strength, cowards may pass for heroes, and faith for falsehood.*

–Aaron Hill

If you have a religious faith, keep it, hold it, grow it, and strengthen it. It can be a great source of inner strength, peace, and stability. It also can give you a sense of self-worth you won't find anywhere else. That inner strength and sense of self-worth can support you during any difficult time in your life, not just during adolescence.

Your religious faith may not be the same as mine. That's OK. My story would be incomplete if I didn't include a chapter describing how my religious faith helped me survive my teen and preteen years, but you can choose whether you want to read this chapter, or choose which sections are most appropriate or helpful for you.

If you're unsure whether you have a religious faith, or you think you want a faith, don't be afraid to explore and discover a religious faith for yourself. Remember in your search that faith is often a lifelong process, not necessarily a single sermon or a message on which you can judge whether religious faith has meaning for you. Religious faith is more about what's on the inside—your inside—than on the way a particular place of worship or service looks or feels. Above all, find a place of worship that has meaning for you, one that you'll *want* to return to on at least a weekly basis.

I was fortunate in my youth to be brought up by parents who believed in attending church regularly. Some people might call that an inherited faith, but I thank my parents and thank God for giving me that gift. Without their gift, I might not have a religious faith today.

Attending church regularly gave me a big emotional boost. How? Maybe it was a smile and a handshake I often received from one of our youth leaders. Maybe it was the sunlight streaming in through the skylight at the peak of our church. Maybe it was my pastor, who frequently made a point of saying hello, asking how I was doing, and sometimes even giving me a big bear hug. He had an entire congregation to think about, but he made sure I knew he cared about me. Wow! That felt great!

My church was like home and family. It was small enough that you knew many of the people in the church but big enough to have enough parents volunteering their time and talents for the youth of the congregation. It had a warm, cozy feeling and a familiarity that was comforting, especially in times when I was confused, lonely, and depressed.

More than handshakes, sunlight, hugs, and a cozy feeling, though, I think my pastor's sermons helped me the most. Our pastor was an inspirational and motivational speaker, and that inspiration was critical to me during my teen years. His speaking voice was dynamic and emotional—not in a fire-and-brimstone kind of way but in an inspiring and uplifting way. The focus for most of his sermons, and his ministry in general, was God's love for us.

During the dark times of depression in my teens, I looked forward to a weekly sermon that reminded me, no matter how bad things got, that God still loved me and cared about me. Those were words I desperately needed to hear when my self-esteem and self-perception were low. Through my pastor's sermons and the words of scripture, I knew that at least someone—God—would love me no matter what I looked like and whether or not anyone else loved me.

Religion and Teenagers

A study of high school seniors has shown that those who attend religious services and participate in religious-based youth groups are more likely than nonattending seniors to:

+ Be proud of themselves.
+ Have a feeling of positive self-worth.
+ Feel a sense of purpose for their lives.
+ Have hope for their future.

Source

The National Study of Youth and Religion.
Smith, Christian. Faris, Robert. 2002.
http://www.youthandreligion.org/publications/docs/Attitudes.pdf
The National Study of Youth and Religion (NSYR) (www.youthandreligion.org) is under the direction of its principal investigator, Dr. Christian Smith, of the Department of Sociology at the University of Notre Dame. The NSYR is generously funded by the Lilly Endowment Inc. of Indianapolis, IN. The NSYR retains all rights to control access to and use of all NSYR data.

Once each week I could count on hope and a positive thought. Once each week, at least for an hour, I could love myself and believe in myself. Quite often those positive feelings faded as the school week progressed and I faced both my troubles and bullies again, but at least once each week my faith and hope were restored.

Our pastor, with his incredible, positive sermons, was one of the most influential people in my early life. His spiritual leadership and my faith were two of the foundations that pulled me through my darkest times. My religious faith was the foundation on which I built strength and hope for the future. Through it, I knew God was with me and he loved me. If your faith can be a foundation for you, it can help you to persevere even when it seems the weight of the world is upon you.

The pastor of the church where I grew up has been the pastor there for fifty years now, and he has been an ordained minister for longer than that. He baptized me as a baby, married my wife and I, and baptized our two children, bringing our life in the church full circle. Having that sense of stability has always been a comfort. We live in a different state now and attend a different church that we also love dearly, but the foundation of faith laid down for me in my childhood lasts to this day.

If you are trying to build a religious faith, maybe even looking for a place of worship like the one I had, I have a few helpful hints. Consider them guideposts for your faith journey (see sidebar).

Guideposts for Your Faith Journey

Live in the Real World

Some people become so absorbed in their faith that they forget to live in the real world and serve the needs of other people in the real world. Although faith can be a great help to you, faith is not only about you and your needs. It is also about the needs of people in your community and the world.

Faith Isn't Jewelry

Some people wear their religious faith like jewelry, put on for show and appearances. A faith that is on the outside will never support you from the inside. Only having and practicing a faith that supports and strengthens you from the inside will help you through the trying times of your life, both now and as an adult.

Stand on Your Faith, Don't Lean on It

Some people use religious faith as a crutch, using it only during a time of trouble, then giving it up again when it doesn't seem to help them. If you use faith as a temporary support instead of using it to help you solve your problems or survive them, has it really helped you? Faith should be a granite foundation upon which you build a life, not a flimsy, temporary crutch you pull out and use when you think you need it. Unless it is part of who you are, who you *really* are on the inside, it cannot be a foundation to help you in times of need.

Live Your Faith

Some people can talk the talk of their faith, but they don't walk the walk. Some people profess to be a Christian and can quote Bible passages left and right, but they treat people around them like dirt under their feet. These people don't really understand the faith. They're not walking the walk. For your faith to support you, it cannot just be words; it must also be actions and a way of living your life.

If faith is the foundation, then scripture is the mortar that binds the foundation together into a strong support. One passage from scripture, the Beatitudes, was particularly helpful to me during my teen and preteen years.

> *Blessed are the poor in spirit*
> *for theirs is the kingdom of heaven.*
> *Blessed are they that mourn*
> *for they shall be comforted.*
> *Blessed are the meek*
> *for they shall inherit the earth.*
> *Blessed are they who hunger and thirst for*
> *righteousness*
> *for they shall be satisfied.*
> *Blessed are the merciful*
> *for they shall obtain mercy.*
> *Blessed are the pure in heart*
> *for they shall see God.*
> *Blessed are the peacemakers*
> *for they shall be called sons of God.*
> *Blessed are those who are persecuted for*
> *righteousness' sake*
> *for theirs is the kingdom of heaven.*
> *Matthew 5:1–10 (Revised Standard Version)*

Each of the sentences from the Beatitudes seemed to be speaking personally to me during my teen and preteen years.

"Blessed are the poor in spirit, for theirs is the kingdom of heaven." I was definitely poor in spirit much of the time, especially during times of mild depression. These words told me that God recognizes and knows those who are poor in spirit, and he has a special place in his heart for them. Like a loving parent, he knew me and cared about me during the darker times in my life.

"Blessed are they that mourn, for they shall be comforted." Although mourning is usually used in the context of death or loss, to me this verse also meant that God would comfort me for the sadness and loneliness that I felt. He knew my pain, and he would comfort me.

"Blessed are they who hunger and thirst for righteousness, for they shall be satisfied." When I was a teen and preteen, I thought this meant that everyone who sought justice would find it. Every time a bully hit me or threatened me, every time someone called me a name, I wanted justice, and this verse gave me comfort that I would get justice. Now I realize that it refers to our own personal efforts to achieve righteousness—living our lives as God would want us to live them. Maybe I didn't understand it correctly then, but it helped me anyway. Now that I understand it better, it helps me even more.

"Blessed are the pure in heart, for they shall see God." This verse reminds me of the times I was picked on and ridiculed by bullies for being a "goody two-shoes." I was trying to live an honest life, trying as best I could not to lie, swear, or treat people poorly. My morals and values seemed contrary to popular culture, and they were certainly fuel for bullies, but this verse told me I was on the right track. I was doing the right thing.

"Blessed are the meek, for they shall inherit the earth." This verse of the Beatitudes meant more to me than all the others. I was shy and quiet, and I was often the target of bullies because of that shyness. "Blessed are the meek," told me I was OK. In fact, God has a special place in his heart for the meek. He says, "they shall inherit the earth." I'm still not sure what "inherit the earth" means in this context, but I believe it means that the meek will be blessed abundantly, beyond what we expect to receive or deserve. For me, it has been true. Despite society's tendency to ridicule the meek, I've been blessed with so many gifts and talents and so much love that it has exceeded my expectations. God has a special place in his heart for the meek.

© Zits Partnership, King Features Syndicate. Reprinted with permission.

There is a quote from Romans that is also very meaningful to me when I look back on my adolescent years:

> *We rejoice in our sufferings, knowing that suffering produces endurance, and endurance produces character, and character produces hope, and hope does not disappoint us, because God's love has been poured into our hearts through the Holy Spirit which has been given to us.*
> *Romans 5:3–5 (Revised Standard Version)*

In the book of Romans, the apostle Paul was writing about the suffering and persecution that early Christians experienced, but the words are just as true for any type of suffering and persecution. Our experiences, both good and bad, shape the kind of person we become later in life, sometimes sooner rather than later. I know that the experiences I had years ago have shaped who I am today. I believe I'm stronger and have greater emotional endurance as an adult than I would have had without the suffering I experienced back then.

Of course, no one wants to feel suffering and persecution. I didn't want it, and I'm sure you don't either. But it helps to know that there is a very positive side effect: the building of strength, endurance, character, and hope.

Knowing that you have survived suffering or persecution makes any future difficulty more manageable (strength and endurance). You begin to take troubles more in stride because you can say to yourself, "If I got through that, I can get through this." We know we can endure because we *have* endured.

Because we know we can endure, we are strengthened by that knowledge, and we are more sensitive and understanding of others who experience suffering and persecution. Both the strength of our character and the nature of our character are altered by the experience. It may seem like a paradox, but we become at the same time stronger and more caring as a result of suffering and persecution.

The knowledge that we can survive, and that we have grown in strength and character because we survived, gives us hope for the future. Hope allows us to keep going, keep moving ahead, and keep having faith.

As I examine who I am as an adult, I can see how my experiences gave me all these positive side effects. Endurance, strength of character, and hope have all come into use at various times in my adult life. For example, when at times my career wasn't going the way I wanted it to, I didn't sit back and whine and complain and blame other people for my predicament. Instead, I took charge and made a change, searching confidently for a job that would be more satisfying and rewarding. It took endurance, strength, and hope to make major changes when they needed to be made. It would have been far easier to sit back, do nothing, and place the blame on other people.

Endurance has shown itself in my life in other ways, too. It has led to a feeling that things always turn out for the best and that "if it wasn't meant to be, it wasn't meant to be." In everything from not getting a job I wanted to having my writing rejected by a publisher, endurance has helped me. When I experienced those rejections, at first I felt disappointed, even hurt, but eventually the strength and endurance I developed as a teen and preteen helped me to take it in stride, put it in perspective, and move on to what was, ultimately, a better outcome anyway.

Another short passage from the Bible has helped me immensely as an adult. I wish I would have known it when I was a teenager; I think it would have helped me then, too. Before I show you the passage, let me explain the background that led up to the day I discovered it's meaning for my life.

When my children were toddlers, we went through the roughest cold and flu season I have ever experienced in my life. From mid-January all the way through the end of February, we shared and passed around one cold or virus after the next. These were the knock-down, drag-out, make-you-feel-miserable kinds of illnesses. At one point during that month and a half, three out of four of us were on antibiotics at the same time for sinus or bronchial infections brought on by the colds and flu.

If you're a parent reading this book, you'll know what I mean. We were awake with one toddler or the other half the night, and the other half of the night we couldn't sleep ourselves because we weren't feeling well. I think the severe lack of sleep made our colds even worse and more difficult to get over. I have never felt so exhausted and miserable for so many consecutive days in my life.

By mid-February, I was at the end of my rope. I was sick and tired of being sick and tired. I prayed and prayed, multiple times per day, asking God to heal us and make us feel better, but we kept on being sick and feeling miserable. My prayers took on an angry tone. I wondered why God wasn't listening. I questioned the belief that "God answers prayer."

Toward the end of February I had a crisis of faith. I stopped praying altogether, and I blamed God for not answering my prayers. I was angry. My faith was drained out of me. I remember going to church the following Sunday. I was grumpy and cranky that day, not only because I was short on sleep, but also because I was angry with God. I could barely bring myself to go to church that day.

That Sunday, one of the Bible lessons read during the service contained this passage:

> *Every test that you have experienced is the kind*
> *that normally comes to people. But God keeps his*
> *promise and he will not allow you to be tested beyond*
> *your power to remain firm; at the time you are put*
> *to the test, he will give you the strength to endure it,*
> *and so provide you with a way out.*
> 1 Corinthians 10:13 (Good News Bible,
> Today's English Version)

It was a revelation for me. God will not test me beyond my power to persevere. In fact, he will give me the power and strength to endure it. Everything I am experiencing happens to other people too. I haven't been singled out for misery; I'm just a human experiencing what *all* humans experience in this life, and God will give me the strength to survive it.

In the context of Chapter 10 of 1 Corinthians, Paul is talking about the test of temptation, the temptation of immorality and the worship of idols. For me, though, the testing was in the context of emotional and spiritual tests—times of trial and tribulation in our lives like the one I was in the midst of that Sunday and the ones I experienced during my teenage years. I realize I've taken the passage slightly out of context, but I believe in this context, the meaning is still powerful, appropriate, and personal.

I realized that day what should have been obvious to me before: We don't live in the Garden of Eden. We live in a world where we may get sick, we may have low self-esteem, we may get picked on and bullied and ridiculed, but God is with us, strengthening us anyway. God gives us the strength to hang in there despite the trials and stresses that *all* people experience. We are not in it alone. We all experience the pains of life, and it is during those times of pain and adversity that God is with us the most.

That day I stopped blaming God for any sickness or problem I faced, and I have never blamed Him since. I realized that Sunday that God gave me the strength to survive a long time ago. As a teen and preteen I survived name calling, bullying, insensitive rejections, and mild depression. God had given me the gift of inner strength, a strength I didn't realize I had at the time, but a strength that I used every day nevertheless.

God answered my prayers that Sunday, not with immediate healing as I had asked, but with a revelation of understanding. He gave me a knowledge, understanding, and strength that I will take with me for the rest of my life.

Each of us can have a crisis of faith at some time in our lives. Maybe you were hoping and praying to get on a sports team at school, but you messed up during tryouts and didn't make the team. Maybe you've been praying for your parents to get along better, but they're getting divorced. Maybe you have been asking God for inner strength, but you just aren't feeling it yet. Maybe you have a chronic disease or a debilitating physical condition and you've been praying for a miracle cure, but it hasn't come. A crisis of faith can happen any time we have a desperate need that seems to go unmet.

We may not receive a miracle to solve our problems, but as 1 Corinthians shows us, we have already been given the strength to persevere, survive, and even thrive despite our situation. Having that strength doesn't necessarily mean your problems will go away. It means that when difficult times occur in your life—and they will—God can give you the strength to wade through the frigid, dark waters until you find yourself once again walking in the sun.

God will give you the strength you need to survive and thrive during your teen and preteen years. All you have to do is ask and believe.

Your Thoughts

✦ If you have a religious faith, how has it helped you so far during your teen and preteen years? What aspects of faith or scripture give you the most support and strength?

✦ Have you ever had a crisis of faith? Think about what was at the heart of that crisis. Did you blame God for giving you the pain you felt or at least not saving you from it? Grief and pain are part of life. Instead of blaming God, think about the ways God can help you get through it.

✦ Do you have favorite quotes from scripture that help lift you up when you are down or in need of support? Write those quotes down in a journal or diary or place them around your bedroom so you'll see them often. When you're struggling with a problem in life, pick out one or two of your favorite passages. Study them and gain strength from them.

Group Discussion

✦ What fundamental concepts and beliefs from your religious faith can help someone who is struggling with the stresses and troubles of life? Is it the love of God? Forgiveness? Why do they help someone who is struggling?

✦ A crisis of faith can be a turning point for an individual, resulting in a turn away from or toward God. What might you say to someone who is experiencing a crisis of faith? Don't choose simplistic sayings. Dig deeper. Use scripture and core elements of your faith to come up with helpful and meaningful things to say.

✦ In small groups, discuss how your faith has helped you through a difficult time in your life. Open up to each other and be honest. Sharing your faith and your struggles with others can strengthen your own faith, and you'll find you are not as alone in your troubles as you thought you were.

14

Gifts and Talents

The best place to succeed is where you are with what you have.

–Charles M. Schwab

Name one or two things you do really well. It doesn't matter what they are: singing, playing football, mathematics, or playing video games. Say them out loud, right now. How does it feel when you say them? It feels really good, doesn't it?

Having a talent or a gift for something can be a tremendous source of self-esteem and happiness. It gives us identity, a sense of who we are and where we belong in this world and this life. It gives us a way to feel good about ourselves, even proud of ourselves. Gifts and talents can give us self-esteem when everything else in life seems to be trying desperately to take it away.

My talents were music and academic ability. When everything else seemed to be going wrong in my life, on days when I felt worthless, I had these two talents to bring me happiness and a feeling of hope. Even when other sources of self-esteem had vanished, I still knew I had a talent for, and love of, music and learning. Sometimes those were the only things that made me feel good about myself, but it was enough to help me keep going.

You might be saying to yourself, "But I'm not good at anything." Trust me, you are. You might not have discovered what your gifts and talents are yet, but they are there, waiting to be discovered.

I believe every person has a talent or gift within him, whether he knows it or not. Often the talent or gift is obvious; it jumps out and stares you in the face without doubt or disguise: The basketball player who always scores the most points per game, the student who always gets straight As, the child singer starring on Broadway, the chess player who wins every tournament.

Sometimes, however, a talent or gift is not so obvious. For most of us, it can take years for a faint hint of interest to grow and mature into a true talent. Writers, engineers, doctors, scientists and elite athletes don't become successful overnight. They might have the basic talent from the beginning, but it can take years of training and refinement to make it visible and apparent.

For some people, their natural gifts and talents are neither obvious nor hinted at, but that doesn't mean the gifts aren't there, waiting to be discovered. All it takes is the right opportunity to bring them out.

Finding a hidden, natural talent is why so many parents, including myself, introduce their children to a variety of activities: soccer, dance, baseball, piano, football, singing, art, scouting, chess, and dozens of others. By exposing their children to many activities, they hope to keep them busy (and hence out of trouble) and to find their children's true talents. Ultimately, this strategy can be beneficial and rewarding for their children because, if the children do find their natural talents, knowing that they have a talent can be a great source of self-esteem, happiness, and direction in their life.

Having said that, though, I have two words of caution. First (and you'll see this echoed again in the next chapter), I believe that if young people are involved in too many activities, they may never get a chance to get very good at any one of them. If you don't have the time to get very good at something, you won't be able to derive much self-esteem from it. Second, if all your activities are focused in one area (such as sports, music, or dance), but you're not enjoying it or improving at it over time, then you may need to broaden your activities to discover your true gifts. You have to discover your own gifts and talents to develop the deep and solid self-esteem that comes from knowing you are really good at something.

Do you need to be involved in sports to develop a sense of teamwork and a healthy competitiveness? Aren't those skills critical for success in our society? You can learn those important skills in more than one way. Playing in a band or orchestra or participating in a debate team or any other team-oriented activity can teach you the value of hard work, dedication, perseverance, working as a team and setting high expectations for yourself. There are many ways to learn the valuable lessons you need to succeed in life.

Another note of caution: Remember that your natural talents, whatever they may be, are a gift. If they are truly natural talents—talents you seemed to have always had—then they are a gift. Don't brag or be arrogant because of them. Don't tease or ridicule people who don't have your particular gift because *everyone* has a gift. Yours may be special, but that doesn't mean you're a better or more important person than someone who has a different gift.

Having a gift or talent, and knowing what it is, helps you to not just succeed in life but also survive those trying times in life that arise all too often. Rely on your gifts and talents as one, but not the only, foundation for your self-esteem and identity during your teen and preteen years.

If you know your best gifts and talents, embrace them with a passion. Be prepared to work hard, though, because refining and perfecting a natural talent takes dedication and hard work. There is a payoff for all that hard work: a strong sense of identity, self-esteem, and hope.

If you don't know what your best talents are, don't be afraid to explore. Exploring to find your talents not only is helpful but also can be great fun. Here are some easy ways to discover and explore your gifts and talents:

- ✦ Look through the community/continuing education course guides offered through your local school district, parks and recreation department, or community college.

If something strikes you as interesting, ask your parent's permission, then sign up for the class. (Be sure to check the minimum age requirements for the course.)

✦ Sign up for a summer camp program.

✦ Get involved in a school, community, or church youth group that focuses on an area of interest to you. See the next chapter of this book for some ideas.

✦ Go to your local library and check out a few books on a topic of interest to you. Think about ways that you might get involved in that area of interest.

✦ Sign up for an elective class at your school, even one that you had never previously considered taking. If nothing else, it will broaden your knowledge and horizons.

✦ Find a person who is a notable figure in your area of interest (e.g., a scientist, politician, teacher, writer, athlete). Find his or her work address or e-mail address from the Internet (it's usually not too hard to do this, especially if the person works for a university or college). Send that person a short, polite letter asking how he or she first got interested in his or her career and what recommendations he or she might have for how to get started in that field. You'll be surprised how willing most people will be to respond personally to a polite letter from a young person. Most people enjoy talking about their professions. When I was a teenager, I wrote a letter to a scientist who was researching ways that future astronauts could use moon rocks to manufacture the materials necessary to build a moon base. I asked him what kind of careers might get me involved in the space program. He wrote a very nice, helpful reply to my letter.

✦ If you are interested in singing, acting, or playing a musical instrument, ask your parents to look into private lessons if you can't get free lessons at school. Be prepared to work hard. When learning to play an instrument it can take several months to a year before you develop your talent enough that it starts feeling more like fun than work.

✦ Ask your parents, aunts, uncles, grandparents, or other relatives what hobbies or side interests they have. Talents and interests often run in families. It doesn't have to be a full-fledged career, either. It can be a hobby like woodworking, painting, model building, photography, craft making, or gardening. Hobbies are relaxing and therapeutic; they can give you joy and a sense of peace throughout your life.

Enjoy your gifts and talents. If you haven't discovered what they are yet, then enjoy your journey to discovery. Discovering and using your given talents is one of the most rewarding and fun things in life. Being good at something, and enjoying spending time doing it, makes all the negative things that happen to us seem both less important and more bearable. Besides our friends and our loved ones, it is our gifts and talents that give meaning and purpose to our lives.

Your Thoughts

✦ Do you already know what your talents and gifts are? Do they give you a sense of self-esteem, hope, and accomplishment?

✦ How have your talents helped you survive your teen or preteen years?

✦ Have you been arrogant or humble with respect to your talents?

✦ If you're not enjoying your current activities or you're not improving at them over time, ask yourself, "Do I need to work harder and apply myself so I can improve and enjoy them more, or is it time to find another activity that might help me to discover my gifts and talents?"

Group Discussion

✦ Does our society focus too much on athletic talent? Is that focus good or bad? In what ways does it help society and in what ways does it hurt it?

✦ What are some talents that might go unnoticed by popular culture and society, but that are still meaningful and important to an individual?

✦ Are young people today overscheduled in too many activities? Why or why not? What positive or negative effects do you think a busy schedule can have on them?

✦ Besides the suggestions in this chapter, what are other ways that someone can discover their gifts and talents?

15

Involvement

*All we need to make us really happy is something
to be enthusiastic about.*

—CHARLES KINGSLEY

You might have heard of scientific studies proving that young people who are involved in sports or other youth organizations get better grades, are less likely to use illegal drugs, and are less likely to engage in dangerous activities than those who are not. All I knew growing up was that being involved in a youth organization was fun; I met new friends, participated in fun activities, and felt a sense of belonging that gave me identity and security.

Looking back now, I realize how involvement in youth organizations helped me to survive my teen and preteen years. When I was feeling lost and didn't like myself, involvement gave me not just a sense of identity and good friendships but also a lot less time to think about how miserable I thought my life was. I had far less time to dwell on the negatives in my life. It forced me to stop wallowing in self-pity—at least for a while—and do something useful and fun with my time.

From my adult perspective, I see there were other benefits too. Every youth organization in which I was involved taught me skills—both tangible and intangible—that I could use for the rest of my life, not just when we met as a group. Citizenship, teamwork, caring for the environment, dedication, hard work, and some of my favorite hobbies are just a few of the things I learned during those years.

As a preteen and early teen, I was involved in a 4-H club, and in high school I was actively involved in a variety of band-related groups. Both organizations were great to belong to, and both had many caring, dedicated, seemingly tireless teachers and parent volunteers. Without the involvement and commitment of parents and teachers, neither organization could have provided the benefits they did to all those involved.

The 4-H organization, contrary to misconception, is not just for farm kids. The only limit to the variety of things you can learn in 4-H is the number of adult volunteers in your club who are willing to teach a skill or craft. My primary areas of focus in 4-H were photography and woodworking. Parent mentors taught us the craft throughout the year, and we had to work hard enough to present our work and be judged at the county fair during the summer. Both photography and woodworking are hobbies I still enjoy to this day—and always will—thanks to the adults in our 4-H club who taught those skills to me.

I believe one of the hallmarks of a great youth organization is its ability to teach young people life skills—skills they can use for the rest of their lives. By learning a life skill, you get not only the short-term enjoyment of learning something new but also the satisfaction and enjoyment of using your skills for many years to come. Remember, as we talked about in the previous chapter, being good at something and knowing that you are good at it can be a tremendous source of self-esteem. Being involved in an organization like 4-H that teaches life skills can be a great way to develop a talent or gift that provides that self-esteem.

Like other youth organizations, 4-H wasn't just a club for having fun, although we did plenty of that too. It was also a place to learn to respect others and respect your community. Several times throughout the year, we participated in community service activities—anything from picking up litter on the side of local streets and highways to helping a local charity. We learned about community and caring while having fun and enjoying fellowship at the same time.

Many youth organizations have sports leagues or special sporting events that allow even not-so-athletic members (like me) a chance to enjoy a team sport in a less competitive environment than school-based sports programs. Our 4-H club participated in softball and basketball tournaments with other local clubs each year. Our club's teams almost always finished in last place, but it didn't matter; we were there to enjoy ourselves and enjoy being with each other. For me, that was perfect. It gave me a chance to enjoy a sport at least a little and to think more positively about sports in general.

By the time of my darkest years in high school, I was no longer involved in 4-H, but I was very involved in music through band-related activities at school. I participated in football and basketball pep bands, marched in local parades, participated in weeklong band trips, competed with other musicians at state competitions, and played in our concert performances. At any given time during the school year, we were busy preparing for a concert, parade, field performance, or competition. It took time and dedication, and I loved every minute of it.

I've mentioned several times in this book how much being involved in band meant to me. It gave me identity, the best of friends, self-esteem, and an emotional outlet through my music. Band and church were the two things that pulled me through my teen years the most. I don't know what I would have done without either of them. It scares me to think about it.

I have my parents to thank for getting me involved in 4-H, music, and church. I think they saw in me a kid who needed not just something to do but somewhere to belong. They were right, and I thank them from the bottom of my heart for nudging me, and sometimes pushing me, to be involved in these organizations. Being involved in them is a big part of why I'm here today and why I'm the person that I am today.

Involvement made a world of difference for me during my teen and preteen years, and I believe it can make a huge difference for you, too. If you're not involved in a youth organization, or you are reconsidering your involvement in your current organization, here are some factors you may want to consider when searching for a youth organization that will be meaningful to you:

+ Will I enjoy myself? This is the number one question. After all, if it isn't fun, then what's the point? Be willing to take a chance, because sometimes you don't know whether you'll enjoy an activity until you try it. I remember that I didn't want to go to our church's high school youth retreats, rejecting my parent's offers to send me for three years in a row. Finally, during my senior year, my parents made me go anyway. At first I was angry with them for not giving me a choice, but as it turned out, I absolutely loved the youth retreat and wished I hadn't missed out on the fun from the previous three years. Sometimes you just have to take a chance and try something new.

+ Does it fit my personality? If you're competitive and athletic, then maybe a sports team is the best fit for you, but if you're not, consider other options as well. Of course, it's difficult to know whether something is a good fit until you've tried it, but think about the other people who are already involved in the organization and how well you'd fit in with them.

+ What will I learn by being involved in the organization? Besides having fun, will I learn character-building traits like teamwork, discipline, dedication, and a sense of community? Will it teach me any life skills? Not every organization will offer all of these rewards, and they don't have to. But if there is a deeper value to being involved than just having fun, you're more likely to enjoy it and benefit from it. If you are trying to decide between two different organizations, you might want to consider the one that teaches you skills you can use for the rest of your life. You'll reap the benefits for years to come.

+ How will I get to meetings or practices? Will I need to walk, carpool, or take public transportation, or will my parents (or other member's parents) be able to take me? If you can only get to meetings or practices sporadically, then you might not be there often enough to enjoy it and to fit in with everyone else.

+ How much does it cost to be involved? Can my parents or I afford my involvement? Some organizations provide scholarships or reduced price membership fees for people with a financial need, so don't be afraid to ask if you need some financial help to join.

+ Am I considering joining an organization only because my friend did or because I feel pressured by my peers to join? What do *I* really want?

Once you've decided on an organization, I recommend the following rule that my parents imposed on my sister and me: You have to stay with the team or organization for an entire season or an entire year. You can't judge how well you'll do or how much you'll like being involved in an organization until you've had time to learn the skills, get to know the other members, fit the involvement into your schedule, and, most importantly, have enough time to get good at it so that you can really begin to enjoy it. This is especially true of any activity that requires mental or physical skill: sports, music, chess, and the like. In addition, this rule will help you learn how to keep commitments, which is an important and valuable life skill in itself.

My parents made only two exceptions to this rule during my youth. In those two cases, my involvement was making me miserable, and we were all terribly disappointed with the way the organizations were run. In both cases, the parents and participants in the organization forgot the real reason for its existence—helping young people to grow and have fun.

If you've given it a year or a season, or you can see there is no way the organization is going to work for you, then don't be afraid to make a change. And don't listen to peers or adults who make you feel guilty for leaving (as long as you've fulfilled any commitments you've made). If the organization isn't right for you, then it isn't right for you. It's your life and your happiness, after all, that are supposed to benefit from being involved in the first place. If all your involvement is doing is making you miserable, then there is no point in continuing. Given the huge number of options available for youth involvement today, there is no reason to stick with an organization that isn't any fun or doesn't help you grow in any way.

Remember, too, that involvement doesn't necessarily have to be a long-term commitment. If you can't afford a yearlong commitment or a time-consuming commitment, look for short courses, workshops, camps, and presentations in areas that interest you. Most museums, zoos, libraries, community colleges, and art and music conservatories offer short courses or workshops for teens where you can learn something new and enjoy being with other people your age who have similar interests. Look at fliers and brochures you receive in the mail or at school, use the Internet, or ask other people if they've heard of any short-term activities in your community.

Another note of caution, and a very important one: Don't let your involvement in extracurricular activities be so all consuming that your grades in school suffer. Make sure you have time to apply yourself and get the best grades you can get. Although being involved in an extracurricular organization can have many benefits, so does a good education—even more so. Good grades mean better jobs and possibly even the luxury of choosing the job you want rather than just settling for any job you can get. You'll only be a teen for seven years, but you'll probably be in the working world for thirty to forty years. If you neglect your education now, you might regret it later. Education is your number one job right now.

If you don't have any ideas for youth organizations you might want to join, the lists on the following pages should give you some ideas.

You can also look at this Internet site: http://directory.google.com/ Top/Kids_and_Teens/People_and_Society/Organizations/. It has a great list of youth organizations broken down by category. If you can't find anything you like there, do some research at your local library or, best of all, ask for recommendations from parents, relatives, teachers, and your peers. They may know an organization that is just right for you.

School-Based Organizations

School-based organizations are probably the most obvious and accessible choice, if they're right for you. If you live in a rural or semirural area with few other options for involvement, these school-based organizations may be worth a look:

✦ Marching band, symphonic band, jazz band, or orchestra.

✦ Choir.

✦ Cheerleading, pom pon, drill team, dance team, color guard.

✦ Chess club.

✦ Football, basketball, volleyball, tennis, track, and other sports.

✦ Intramural sports.

✦ National Honor Society.

✦ Student council.

✦ DECA/Delta Epsilon Chi (marketing, management and business education).

✦ Yearbook, school newspaper, or literary magazine.

✦ Drama club.

✦ Debate club.

✦ Junior Achievement.

✦ Foreign language clubs (for example, French club, German club).

✦ Service clubs.

Fine Arts Organizations

Dance/Ballet

The best way to find information about dance or ballet programs in your area is through friends or teachers at your school. If you know someone who takes dance lessons, ask where he or she takes them. Your school's drama or fine arts teacher might know about dance schools in your area. You can also look in your local Yellow Pages under the category heading "Dancing Instruction."

Youth Orchestra or Chorus

If you play an instrument or sing, check with your local symphony or professional choral organization to see if they have a youth orchestra or choir. If you play a band instrument, you might also find community bands through your local community college or community center. Ask your band or orchestra teacher for suggestions (many teachers play in community or professional bands or orchestras outside of work). Check with your local community theater organization as well; they need instrumentalists to play the music for their musical theater productions.

Worship-Based Organizations and Activities

If you attend a place of worship, chances are they have organized programs for youths:

- ✦ Mission and service trips.
- ✦ Youth club.
- ✦ Sports clubs.
- ✦ Volunteer as a vacation Bible school helper or nursery helper.
- ✦ Food or clothing donation drives.
- ✦ Choir, church band, folk group.
- ✦ Tutoring and mentoring.

Community, Civic, and Fraternal Organizations

Kiwanis International

Kiwanis International (http://www.kiwanis.org/) is an organization dedicated to helping young people. Through Kiwanis, you can be involved in Builders Club at the middle school (or junior high) level or Key Club at the high school level. Both are great organizations that help you to learn about leadership and community service. You can also continue your involvement through Circle K clubs at the college level.

Freemasons Fraternal Organizations

Freemasons organizations date back to the eighteenth century. Today, young people can get involved in Job's Daughters (http://www.iojd.org/) if you are a girl or DeMolay (http://www.demolay.org/) if you are a boy. Be sure to check these websites for an overview of the organizations, as well as eligibility requirements and availability in your area.

Optimist International

The Optimist International (http://www.optimist.org) and the associated Junior Optimist Octagon International, JOOI (http://www. optimist.org/default.cfm?content=jooi/jooi.htm), are dedicated to "Bringing Out the Best in Kids" through community service projects that improve the quality and safety of their local communities. The Optimist organizations' hands-on neighborhood cleanup and beautification projects not only improve neighborhoods but also teach valuable lessons about caring for your community and the world we live in.

Lions Clubs

Lions Clubs are community organizations dedicated to improving the quality of life for people around the world. Although the Lions Club membership is for adults, part of its focus is on youth programs that help educate and improve the lives of young people. You can participate in the Lions Club youth programs through youth camps, youth exchanges, and contests. See http://www.lionsclubs.org/EN/content/youth_index.shtml for more information.

Other Organizations

There are an incredible number of youth organizations that are not school, civic/community, or worship based. You have no doubt heard about many of these such as Boy Scouts, Girl Scouts, and Boys and Girls Clubs of America. It would be impossible to describe all of them here, but the following list should give you a good idea of where to start looking for a youth organization that is right for you.

4-H

You can learn about 4-H through its website: http://www.4-h.org/. If there is a 4-H club in your area, you're in luck, otherwise you might have to consider starting your own club with the help of your parents. One of the great things about 4-H that I didn't mention earlier, is that the *kids* run the meetings, not the parents!

Local Parks and Recreation Departments

Your local, county and state parks and recreation departments can provide a wealth of opportunities to learn new skills and get involved. Check out their activity and course listings to see what is available. Don't limit yourself to your own city or county; many neighboring communities may let you use their facilities too. Most park and recreation departments have both indoor and outdoor facilities where you can learn and enjoy a wide variety of activities:

- ✦ Classes and teams in baseball, soccer, tennis, volleyball, swimming, and fitness.
- ✦ Skate parks and water parks.
- ✦ Classes and facilities for photography, pottery, and painting.
- ✦ Lessons in singing, acting, dancing, and magic.
- ✦ Multicultural and ethnic classes and programs.
- ✦ Volunteer opportunities.
- ✦ Nature and fitness trails.

- ✦ Historic buildings and events or celebrations.
- ✦ Planetariums.
- ✦ Nature and ecology programs.

American Field Service (AFS)

Hosting a foreign student can be both fun and educational. AFS is one of the largest student exchange services, but it's not the only one. My family was involved with AFS and other student exchanges for several years, hosting students from Denmark, Netherlands, South Africa, Finland, and Cyprus. Some of those former students are still good friends with our family.

Even if you don't host a student, you can be involved in the AFS Club at your school, and get to know and socialize with the exchange students. You can learn more about AFS at http://www.afs.org/.

Future Farmers of America (FFA)

If you live in a farming region and are interested in any type of farming as a career, then this might be the organization for you. Like 4-H, there are local clubs you can join (or start). To learn more about FFA, go to http://www.ffa.org/.

Boy Scouts and Girl Scouts

The Boy Scouts of America and Girl Scouts of America have been around for years and years. They are probably the best-known youth organizations in the United States, and they are not just for young children. You can read more about Boy Scouts at http://www.scouting.org/ and Girl Scouts at http://www.girlscouts.org/.

Venture Club

The Boy Scouts organization now also includes the co-ed (both boys and girls) Venture Clubs for young people age fourteen to twenty. If you enjoy the outdoors, this might be a great organization for you. You can read more about Venture Clubs at http://www.scouting.org/venturing.

Explorer's Club (Scouting)

The Boy Scouts organization also includes co-ed Explorer's Clubs for nearly every area of interest: plants and ecology, science, adventure, sailing, and many more. The best way to find one is to do an Internet search for "Explorer's Club" and start looking for one that interests you.

Explorer's Club (Nonscouting)

The Explorer's Club (http://www.explorers.org) is primarily an organization for adults who engage in scientific research and exploration around the globe, but it offers student memberships to young people age sixteen through twenty-four who are attending an accredited high school or college. This Explorer's Club is *not* the same as the scouting-based Explorer's Club, but if you're interested in the natural sciences and exploration, it might be worth a look.

Boys and Girls Clubs of America

Boys and Girls Clubs of America have been around for many years, especially in urban areas. These clubs are a great way to be involved in safe and healthy after school activities. Read about them, or find one in your area, by going to http://www.bgca.org/.

YMCA

If you have a YMCA in your area, it can offer valuable and fun courses on health and fitness. Many also offer youth team sports like volleyball or basketball in a more intramural style than a formal school-based sports program. To find out more about the YMCA and to locate a club in your area, go to http://www.ymca.net/ on the Internet (make sure to type the correct address into your browser, because www.ymca.org is only for the San Diego, California, area, but www.ymca.net is for the entire United States).

Nature and Ecology Organizations

If you are interested in nature, conservation, ecology, or preserving our national parks, you can join a number of organizations. If you can't find local chapters for any of the organizations listed here, do an Internet search for "conservation organizations" or check with your state's conservation department or department of natural resources; they may be able to point you to organizations in your area.

+ Isaak Walton League of America (http://www.iwla.org/)
+ The Nature Conservancy (http://nature.org)
+ The National Park Foundation (http://www.national parks.org/)
+ Students Conserving America (http://www.sca-inc.org/)

Volunteering

Consider volunteering at your local science center, museum, zoo, hospital, or nursing home. Volunteer as a day camp or weeklong camp leader for younger children (through Boy/Girl Scouts, 4-H, Special Olympics [http://www.specialolympics.org/], the Muscular Dystrophy Association [http://www.mda.org/], or others). Sign up for a walk-a-thon.

Volunteering for literacy, English as a second language, or other types of tutoring can be personally rewarding, and it's an important and vital community service. If you are considering becoming a teacher some day, then tutoring might be a great way to learn more about teaching. The best way to find out about tutoring and literacy programs in your area is to ask your teachers about tutoring programs in your school district. You can also find information on the Internet by typing "literacy tutoring" followed by the name of your city or metropolitan area into your favorite Internet search engine. For example, searching for "literacy tutoring St. Louis" will show you the literacy programs in the St. Louis metropolitan area.

Speaking/Debating and Leadership Conferences

Speaking and Debating

If you like speaking, reading poetry, or debating, find out if your school has a debating club or speaking and poetry reading competitions. It's a great chance to get some experience with public speaking.

You can learn more about debating and debate clubs through the International Debate Education Association (http://www.idebate. org/index.php). If you are interested in starting a debate club, take a look at http://www.idebate.org/debate/start_debate_club.php for information and guidelines.

Leadership Conferences

Leadership conferences are a great way to learn leadership skills and have fun at the same time. The list here is a small sampling of organizations involved in youth leadership. Search the Internet or ask parents and teachers to find more.

+ Congressional Youth Leadership Council (http://www. cylc.org/)
+ National Youth Leadership Forum (http://www.nylf.org/)
+ National Youth Leadership Network (http://www.nyln.org/)
+ Youthleadership.com (http://www.youthleadership.com/)
+ People to People Student Ambassadors (http://www.student ambassadors.org/)
+ Washington Workshops (http://www.workshops.org/)

Youth Activism

Many organizations for youth activism are available. Just search the Internet for the phrase "students against" or "students for" to find a sampling. A few are listed here:

Students Against Destructive Decisions (SADD)

Originally founded as Students Against Drunk Driving (http:// www.saddonline.com/), this nationwide organization has expanded its scope to include other destructive behaviors and decisions, such as bullying and teen suicide. You can get involved at your local school and at the national level. Helping other young people deal with the difficult decisions of adolescence is a great way to help you deal with the same issues. Being involved with this organization might give you the perspective you need to help you survive your teen and preteen years, and you'll be helping others to survive as well.

Students Against Violence Everywhere

SAVE (http://www.nationalsave.org/) members learn about resolving conflict, preventing crime, being a good citizen, and promoting nonviolence through school and community service projects, speakers, and training sessions. Safe communities and safe schools are the goals of this organization.

Internships

Internships (working at a real job in your field of interest over your summer break) are a great way to explore an area of interest to see if it is right for you. Internships are a tremendous learning experience. Most internship programs focus on high school- and college-aged students. You can learn about internship programs by contacting corporations and nonprofit organizations directly. The U.S. government also offers a limited number of paid internships (see http://www.studentjobs.gov/ for more information).

As you can see from the information on the previous pages, the variety and number of opportunities for involvement is mind boggling. Somewhere out there is an organization or activity that is just right for you. Get involved, learn something new, and have fun!

Your Thoughts

✦ If you are already involved in an organization, in what ways is your involvement benefiting you, both tangibly (learning new skills) and less tangibly (character development).

✦ What could you get out of your involvement that you're not already getting out of it? What changes might you make to benefit even more from your involvement?

Group Discussion

✦ What are the characteristics of a great youth organization? What should it teach you or do for you?
✦ Discuss good and bad experiences you have had with youth organizations. What was it that made the experience good or bad?

16
Hopes and Dreams

Reach high, for stars lie hidden in your soul.
Dream deep, for every dream precedes the goal.

—PAMELA VAULL STARR

A desperate feeling of hopelessness is what I remember most about the times when I was depressed. How, then, can I tell you to have hope when the feeling of hopelessness can be overwhelming? It's not easy, but we can train ourselves to look for hope—even if it's only a hint of hope—in any situation, no matter how desperate it might seem at the moment.

Hopelessness is born out of a belief that nothing in our lives will change or improve, a belief that we will be saddled with our problems forever. That's how I felt during the valleys of my roller-coaster ride. I believed my life would never change. Worse yet, there was a part of me that believed I deserved all the bad things that happened to me. When you start feeling like that, depression and self-loathing become a vicious circle, each feeding on the other. How did I find hope during these times? I looked for reminders of hope, I set goals, and I dreamed.

Daily Reminders of Hope

When I was a teen and preteen, I had a poster taped to the inside of my bedroom door. I saw it every time I left my room, particularly each morning when I got out of bed. The poster had a picture of magnificent, towering trees in a deep, dense forest. The trees were so tall you could not see their tops; you could only imagine how high they must be. Shafts of golden sunlight sliced through the darkness under the trees providing a religious beauty to the scene. The caption of the poster read—

Today I have grown taller by walking with the trees.

Every time I stopped to look at that poster, I smiled and felt good inside. It reminded me of the grand and awesome beauty of the world around us, and it reminded me of my love of the natural world. The tall trees transported me for a brief moment to a place of peace, serenity, and reflection—even spirituality. The poster reminded me that some things are right with the world. Beauty, purity, and hope do exist.

I gained hope and strength from that poster. I knew that if nothing else went right in my life, I would someday walk with the trees in a forest like that and gape in wonder at the sight. A few years ago, as an adult, I did just that. I walked through a coastal redwood forest in California, craning my neck to look up in search of the tops of trees that were so high I could not make them out. Narrow shafts of sunlight filtered down through the trees just like in the poster. I walked in awe and reverence. My dream came true.

Daily reminders of hope can help us to see hope in our own lives even at times when we feel we no longer have any hope. Try to find an inspirational, hopeful poster to put in your bedroom (and, no, I'm not talking about a poster of the latest teen idol in a skimpy swimsuit or muscle shirt). Place the poster in a prominent, noticeable location in your bedroom. Try to look at it at least once a day. If the poster (or better yet, multiple posters) begins to seem like wallpaper, forgotten and unnoticed, move it somewhere else. Our eyes notice change—you will start looking at it more often again.

Books can serve as reminders, too. An aunt of mine once bought me a book of inspirational sayings called *Wings of Silver* (Jo Petty, Norwalk, CT, C.R. Gibson Company, 2000). It was loaded with useful, helpful words of wisdom and hope. Every time I read it, I got a smile on my face and a warm feeling in my heart. Consider buying a book like that and placing it in an easy-to-remember place in your room, such as on a desktop or the top of a dresser. Remember to read it once in awhile. You don't have to read it all at once—just pick it up from time to time for a short, but important, emotional boost. It can be a great reminder, and builder, of hope.

Consider making your own book of hope. Buy a blank journal from a bookstore in which you can save your favorite words of wisdom as you come across them. You can also use your journal to record compliments and praise you receive from teachers, friends, or anyone else. When you're feeling down about yourself, you can reread those gems and be reminded of your good qualities and skills. Using your journal to record your thoughts and feelings can also be very therapeutic; writing down negative feelings can take away some of their sting.

Photographs are another powerful source of hope and inspiration. Maybe it's a picture of you holding a huge bass you caught on your last fishing trip, a picture of you holding a trophy you won in a competition, or a picture of your favorite place in the world—a park, a lake, or a mountain vista. If you have pictures like that, pull them out of those hidden boxes and drawers where we so often leave these treasures; place a few of them around your room as reminders of the good times in your life. Don't worry; the experiences shown in those photos won't be the only good times in your life.

Pictures that remind us of hope don't necessarily have to be ones that you or a family member took with a camera. A clipping from a newspaper, magazine, or an Internet website can be just as powerful. Maybe it's a stop-action photo of your favorite sports star making an incredible play, an astronaut floating in space with the earth displayed below, or maybe a picture of a famous scientist or writer you admire. Any picture that reminds you of the joys and potential of life can give you the hope you need to help get through a difficult day, week, or year.

As with posters, you may need to rearrange inspirational photos and books in your room from time to time so that you notice them more often. Also, keep your eyes open for new and even better photos, posters, and books; the variety will be refreshing, and searching for new sources of inspiration will keep your mind and heart focused on the positive images of life.

Music can be another, deeply felt reminder of hope. Music is uplifting, refreshing, and rejuvenating. Despite the media attention that angry, hateful music tends to receive, plenty of inspirational, positive music is available. If you have a religious faith, look for spiritual and inspirational music by artists who share your faith. There are also plenty of pop artists whose music has a positive message. All you have to do is look for them. Go to a good music store and browse around. Find a store that lets you listen to selections of an artist's songs so you can select the ones you like the most. The legal, online music download websites are also a great place to sample music. If you have a CD burner, MP3 player, or IPod, you can create your own custom blend of the songs or music that inspire you the most.

If you're afraid your friends will laugh at you for having inspirational music in your collection, then keep those CDs in a special box or drawer so you can pull them out and listen to them when you need a boost. Remember, it's your life and your happiness. Don't let a friend talk you out of listening to the kind of music that helps make your life both bearable and meaningful. Whatever reminders of hope you choose, look at or listen to them often. It's human nature, I believe, to slide back down the slope toward negative thoughts, bitterness, and self-pity. We need frequent and varied sources of inspiration to keep us from sliding down that slope.

Peanuts: © United Feature Syndicate, Inc. Reprinted with permission.

Goals and Dreams

When I was in high school, I wanted to become an astronaut or at least work for NASA's manned space program. When I wasn't doing homework or playing music, I was usually reading about space. I read books about space, magazine articles about space, even free reports and literature from NASA that I requested through the mail from its public information office. I ate it up. I loved it. I often daydreamed about being an astronaut, imagining myself floating in space or walking on the moon or Mars. I imagined all the great and wonderful things I would do and the amazing things I would see.

Was my dream realistic? Maybe, maybe not, but it doesn't matter. The dream energized and excited me. It helped propel me through the toughest times of my teenage years. My dream of becoming an astronaut was one of the foundations that supported me and helped me to keep going when I felt like giving up.

Having a dream can provide an almost constant source of hope. It gives you something to look forward to—the proverbial light at the end of the tunnel. Your dream doesn't always have to be realistic or immediately achievable. It only has to be something you really want and would really enjoy. It should be something that brings a smile to your face and warmth to your heart when you imagine achieving it.

While we're on the topic of hopes and dreams, let's talk about a topic that is central to any hope or dream: Knowing who you are. You have to know, and accept, who you are—what you enjoy about life, what makes you happy, what makes you tick, what you like to do with your time, what you believe in, and what you don't. It's what Dr. Phillip McGraw ("Dr. Phil") calls "Your Personal Truth" or your authentic self in his book *Self Matters: Creating Your Life from the Inside Out* (Phillip C. McGraw, Ph.D., New York: Simon & Schuster, 2001).

Let me give you a few examples of my own personal truths. First, I could never be a salesperson; by that I mean the kind that will sell anything and make up any kind of lie to make a sale. I've known people like that (I even kicked one out of my house once). That's not me, and it never will be. If I lied to myself and took a job in sales I would hate it, no doubt about it.

That goes for being a manager, too. When you're managing other workers, your responsibilities are often abstract and intangible. I need tangible, detailed work, work in which I can see clearly at the end of each day what I've accomplished and why it was important (which is probably why I enjoy writing computer software and writing books). That's just who I am, and I know it.

Of course, there's nothing wrong with being a salesperson or manager, unless your personal truth is that you hate being a salesperson or manager (or doctor, lawyer, or any other profession). If you aren't being true to yourself, you will probably make yourself miserable.

What about other personal truths? Do you feel pressured by your parents or friends to be involved in a sport you don't even enjoy? Are you expected to go to the same college or university your parents attended or get a college degree in a field for which you have no interest? Do you feel forced to work for your parent's company after high school, but you don't want to? If you have given in to pressures like these and are playing at being someone you are not, is it making you happy? Probably not.

What does this have to do with your hopes and dreams? If the hopes and dreams you are pursuing are someone else's hopes and dreams for your future, those "forced" hopes and dreams will not help you get through your teenage years. In fact, they can make those years even more difficult. For your hopes and dreams to guide and support you, they have to be your own.

Now, I'm not telling you to quit the football team or go "tell off" your parents. There are times when our parents really do know what's best for us. They might even understand our own personal truths, our own inner self, better than we do, so give them the benefit of the doubt. But—and this is an important "but"—if you give your parents' or anyone else's guidance and direction your best, most honest effort, but it just isn't working for you, then you need to tell them that. If their hopes and dreams for you are only making you unhappy, even miserable, then you have to speak out in a polite, respectful, and mature way. If you're not honest with yourself and everyone else about who you are, then it will probably lead to pain and resentment. And that doesn't do anyone any good.

If you're being honest with your true self, and you have some inkling of dreams or goals for your life, do you have to limit yourself to just one goal or dream? No, you don't. Why not have several—some more short term and realistic, others longer term and more challenging? That way, when you feel discouraged or doubtful about one goal, you can dream about achieving the others.

Remember, it's OK to change your mind too. Don't feel guilty if you are no longer interested in a goal or dream you once had. It's OK to abandon or change it. It's your dream, so do with it what you want: nurture it, dump it, revise it, or set it aside for a while. It's your choice, because it's your dream. Also, remember this: If your dream doesn't come true, that doesn't mean you are a failure. Maybe your dream just needs a little revising, clarification, or a new direction. Maybe it's time to set it aside and focus on a new dream. Regardless of whether it comes true or not, a dream can give you hope for the future. Because of that hope, dreaming is never a waste of time.

You don't have to share your dreams with anyone if you don't want to, either. If you think people will laugh or poke fun at your aspirations, then keep them close to your heart. It can still be your dream—your secret source of inspiration—even if no one else knows about it.

If you do share your dream with someone, and he or she doesn't "get it," don't be discouraged. Don't give up on your dream just because someone else doesn't understand it or doesn't believe you can achieve it (even if it's a parent or your best friend). Often, people measure our dreams against their own perspective, so it's common to face skepticism and doubt from a friend or acquaintance. When I told a friend about my dream of writing a book—this book—he laughed out loud at me. His reaction made me feel angry and hurt. He judged my dream by his own expectations and experiences, not by mine. As you can see by reading this book, I didn't give up on my dream of writing just because he didn't "get it." If your dream is real to you, then it is real, no matter what anyone else says. Just because someone else doesn't understand it or appreciate it doesn't mean you can't achieve it.

What types of goals or dreams can provide you with the hope and inspiration you need to get you through the difficult times of life? Almost any dream will do, if your dream inspires you to try harder and to persevere. In addition, goals that require real effort and dedication on your part are the ones that will be the most rewarding when you finally achieve them. You might have a dream of meeting and dating a particular boy or girl, but you should avoid pinning all your hopes on that type of goal. Your hope for the future needs to be built on a solid foundation, not just a single short-term, shaky pillar.

The following two-part exercise is designed to energize your vision for your dreams, both short-term and long-term:

Brainstorming Your Short-Term Goals

Write a list of realistic short-term goals for yourself. Don't just think about goals: write them down on paper or type them into a computer. You don't necessarily have to know how you are going to achieve these goals right now, but they should be realistic and exciting or inspirational to you. Use the following examples to guide you, but choose your own short-term goals. Be specific and clear when writing them.

✦ Set a goal to beat your personal best time in a sport. Set a specific time and strive for it.

✦ If your band or orchestra has a competitive chair program, set a goal of moving up one or two chairs in rank, maybe even reaching first chair for your instrument, if that is within reach.

✦ Choose a challenging piece of music and master it.

✦ Think of a class in school that is difficult for you. Set a goal to raise your grade by a whole letter grade, for example from a C to a B or a B to an A.

✦ Run for class president, or become the leader of another school organization such as debate club, honors society or chess club.

✦ If you've considered joining a sports team at school, but haven't had the courage to try out, set a goal of getting on the team the next time it has tryouts.

✦ If you enjoy acting, or have always wanted to try it, set a goal to prepare for and audition for your school's next play or musical production.

✦ Volunteer at your local animal shelter.

✦ Write an article for the school newspaper.

✦ Redesign your bedroom.

✦ Learn to ski, surf or skateboard.

Brainstorming Your Long-Term Goals (or Dreams for Your Life after High School)

In this exercise, explore longer-term goals for yourself. Write on paper or type a list of goals or dreams that might take months to achieve, years to achieve, or even a lifetime to achieve. The timing doesn't matter; just brainstorm goals for your life that get you excited. If you catch yourself writing a goal or dream but then erasing it because you don't think it's realistic, or you're afraid someone else won't think it's realistic, stop! Don't erase it! It doesn't matter how difficult or unrealistic a goal may seem; this brainstorming exercise is all about getting excited about your future and what you might do with your life. That excitement is the fuel that will drive you forward.

Use the following list of examples to help stimulate your goal writing, but be sure to write goals that are your own. As with the short-term goals, be clear and specific.

+ Be a doctor.
+ Become a teacher.
+ Be an architect; design your own home, design amazing and beautiful buildings.
+ Get on the Olympic team for the next Olympics.
+ Learn to fly an airplane.
+ Run a marathon, complete a triathlon, complete an open-water swim.
+ Take up rock climbing or mountain climbing as a hobby.
+ Write a book.
+ Run for public office.
+ Hike the Appalachian Trail.
+ Become a paleontologist and discover a fossilized species that no one has discovered before.
+ Learn a second language (or maybe even a third).
+ Start your own business.
+ Plan a trip to Europe or another destination beyond the borders of your country.
+ Become a scientist or engineer. Invent new fuels or technology that will revolutionize the world.

As soon as you finish brainstorming your goals, take a moment to think how you felt while writing them. It felt good, didn't it? Having hopes and dreams is exciting, motivating and fulfilling. By writing your goals you've taken the first step into your *own* future, a future that you can determine.

Pick your favorite one, two or three short-term goals and begin making plans for how you will achieve them. Pick your top long-term goal and think about what you could be doing even now to start preparing the path to that dream. As I mentioned earlier, don't give up and don't be afraid to change your goals and dreams. After all, they're your goals, your dreams.

Dreams, to a great extent, define us. They shape us, mold us, and direct us. They make us grow to achieve more, and be more, than we ever thought we could be. Dreams focus our minds on things larger and grander than ourselves. They channel our minds to the future rather than the present and, as a result, they take our minds away from the troubles and pain of the present. Dreams have no room for self-pity. Dreams have no room for self-doubt.

As for my dream of becoming an astronaut, it never came true. I have never worked for NASA, either. Fate and life's many choices have led me down another path. Although my dream of becoming an astronaut never came true, I don't believe my dream was in vain or a waste of time. That dream was a treasure trove of hope during a time in my life when I needed it most. For that reason, it was priceless.

Who knows . . . maybe someday, a few decades from now, you'll be watching a news program about tourists in space, and you'll see a gray-haired old guy with a huge smile on his face, waving to the camera as he floats around in a space station. Maybe, just maybe, that will be me waving at you. After all, I can always dream.

And so can you.

Your Thoughts

+ Keep the goals and dreams you just brainstormed in a journal or another safe place. Go back and read them from time to time to be reinspired and see which ones have come true.

+ Have you ever laughed or scoffed at someone when he or she told you about a dream? Why did you do that? Were you judging your friend by your own standards and beliefs? How can you support him (or her) even if you don't believe the dream is realistic?

✦ Much of this chapter has focused on short- and long-term goals and dreams, but what about extremely short-term goals, such as "I just want to survive today." When I woke up in the morning on days like that, I tried to think of at least one thing to look forward to during the day, even if it was only that my mom was making homemade lasagna for dinner that night (one of my favorites!). Think about the types of events or situations you can look forward to on *any* given day and think of at least one of them each morning when you wake up. It feels great to begin a difficult day with a happy thought.

Group Discussion

✦ What are some techniques for achieving a goal or dream? How can you make a seemingly impossible dream seem more achievable and believable?

✦ Discuss any experiences you might have had when you shared your goals and dreams with a friend or parent. Were they receptive and supportive or skeptical and critical? How did their reaction make you feel?

✦ What criticism or skepticism do you think dreamers throughout history have faced (for example, the Wright brothers, early rocket scientists, Antarctic explorers, mountain climbers, and the like)? Do you think people thought they were crazy?

✦ Why are some people inherently dreamers while others have their feet firmly on the ground? What are the pros and cons of being either a dreamer or a nondreamer?

17
Where Do I Go from Here?

The great thing in this world is not so much where
we are, but in what direction we are moving.

—OLIVER WENDELL HOLMES

Where do you go from here? You now know seven major ways to survive your teen and preteen years, and you've seen dozens of individual strategies within those seven major categories. But how do you put them into action in your life? How do you smooth out the roller-coaster ride? How can you have hope and faith for your future?

Write down a plan.

It's a simple, yet extremely powerful technique: Write down a plan of what you want to achieve, why you want to achieve it, and the changes and steps you will use to make it happen. Henriette Anne Klauser, in her book *Write It Down, Make It Happen: Knowing What You Want—and Getting It!* (New York: Scribner, 2000), introduced me to this technique, and I'm a believer. As Klauser describes in her book, writing down what we want in life—our goals, hopes, and dreams—and *why* we want it commits it to memory, making our minds more attuned to seeing ways to make it happen. Because we know what we want and why we want it, we begin to see ways to get it. Using this technique, I was able to plan small, but important steps to make this book (my first) a reality. Knowing what you want and breaking the goal into smaller, more manageable steps helps us to see *how* we can get from where we are to where we want to be. It worked for me; it can work for you too.

Start by reviewing the seven survival strategies described in this book. From those, extract at least ten specific actions you can take to help yourself survive or change. Don't write down vague goals like "I need to deal with bullies better." Rather, write down specific actions you will take such as:

✦ When bullies taunt me or pick on me, I will ignore them and walk away, if I can. I won't give them the satisfaction of a reaction. If that doesn't solve the problem, I will go to an adult for help, such as my parents or a school counselor.

✦ When bullies tease me, laugh at me, or hurt me, I will remind myself that they have a problem, not me.

✦ I will purchase an inspirational poster and hang it in my room.

✦ I will purchase an inspirational book that I will place in a prominent place in my room and read frequently.

✦ I will forgive myself for the embarrassing mistakes I make.

✦ I will forgive my parents for the mistakes that they make.

✦ This week I will make an appointment to talk with my school's counselor.

✦ Every time a girl (or boy) rejects me, I will write the following down on a piece of paper: "Somewhere in this world is a person who is right for me. I just haven't found that person yet."

✦ I will add the word "yet" to the end of every negative sentence I say about myself.

✦ I will try to view life as a series of lessons—some easy, some hard—so I don't get so stressed out about events that are frustrating or out of my control.

✦ When I feel frustrated, anxious, or embarrassed by some event or situation in my life, I will ask myself, "Will I care about this problem a few months from now? A year from now?" If the answer is no, then I'll try to not get so upset about it.

If there aren't enough applicable examples in this book, invent some of your own. Better yet, talk with parents, relatives, or adult friends to find out how they survived their teen and preteen years. What strategies did they use? What words of wisdom helped them? Did they have trouble with bullies or low self-esteem? If so, how did they deal with their problems? If you're tired of your parents asking you questions, here is your chance to turn things around—have them answer *your* questions.

Once you have a specific list of strategies in mind, write them down and start thinking of ways to make them happen. If you are diligent and try hard, you'll notice a difference. If your chosen strategies don't work, don't get discouraged; pick other strategies, write them down, and continue trying. Whatever you do, don't give up. Keep trying. Keep moving in the right direction.

What should you do if you don't think any of this will help you? All I can do is offer myself, and possibly millions of other adults (maybe even your parents), as examples of people who made it through difficult, trying adolescent years to reach adulthood. I'm so glad I did, because I discovered a wonderful, rewarding, and love-filled life as an adult.

Can I guarantee that your life will turn out as well as mine did? Can I guarantee that you will see the night-and-day difference I saw when I became an adult? No, I can't. Do I know what the future has in store for you? No, I don't. Do I know what the future has in store for me? No, I don't know that either. Life offers no guarantees.

Uncertainty about the future drives much of human activity. We purchase insurance in case something happens to our car or home; we buy extended product warranties in case things break down; we wear seatbelts and drive cars with airbags, not because we know we'll need them, but "just in case" we do. Sometimes I wish there was a way to predict the future—some way to eliminate the uncertainty and fear in our lives—but with that certainty we would lose pleasant surprises, serendipitous discoveries, and thousands of other joys in life that only come from experiencing them for the first time. Life is full of first-time treasures: learning to ride a bike, getting your driver's license, kissing, falling in love, holding your child's hand for the first time. Such moments are priceless. They make life worth living, and I wouldn't trade them for anything, not even for the certainty of knowing my future.

Although our futures are uncertain, I can guarantee one thing: If you don't get through your teen and preteen years, you will never be able to discover the joys and gifts that life has waiting for you in adulthood. Your life is a gift worth waiting for, even worth struggling for if necessary. If your life transforms half as much as mine did, you'll be glad you did whatever you had to do to get through your teenage years.

Hang in there. Don't give up. Keep trying. Have faith. Get through your adolescent years with whatever strategies work for you. Enjoy and live the gift of life to its fullest. Your life is more precious and rare than the most precious diamond. And every second of it is yours. *All yours.*

Positive Quotations

ositive, inspirational, and motivational quotations can be just what we need to help us through a difficult moment or a challenging day. They can also guide us throughout our lives. The following pages contain positive quotations that I found while writing this book. Read one each day or whenever you need an emotional boost.

If you would like more quotations, look at your library or bookstore for books of quotations or inspirational poetry. In my opinion, one of the best quotation books is *The Book of Positive Quotations*, compiled and arranged by John Cook (New York: Gramercy Books, 1999). Keep your eyes open for other sources of quotations, too. When you find a quote you like, write it in a journal or in the blank pages at the end of this book. It's amazing how a few words of wisdom can change your perspective or give you the strength to get through a tough time in your life.

Courage and Perseverance

Endure, and preserve yourselves for better things.
—Virgil

We win half the battle when we make up our minds to take the
world as we find it, including the thorns.
—Orison S. Marden

The race is not always to the swift, but to those
who keep on running.
—Anonymous

Far better is it to dare mighty things, to win glorious triumphs,
even though checkered by failure . . . than to take rank with those
poor souls who neither enjoy much nor suffer much, because they
live in that gray twilight that knows not victory nor defeat.
—Theodore Roosevelt

What lies behind us and what lies before us are tiny matters
compared to what lies within us.
—Ralph Waldo Emerson

He conquers who endures.
—Persius, Roman satirist (34 AD–62 AD)

If you want the rainbow, you gotta put up with the rain.
—Dolly Parton

When you get to the end of your rope, tie a knot and hang on.
—Franklin Delano Roosevelt

Giving up is the ultimate tragedy.
—Robert J. Donovan

If you want to see the sun shine, you have to weather the storm.
–FRANK LANE

I find that it is not the circumstances in which we are placed, but the spirit in which we face them, that constitutes our comfort.
–ELIZABETH T. KING

Reach high, for stars lie hidden in your soul.
Dream deep, for every dream precedes the goal.
–PAMELA VAULL STARR

The great thing in this world is not so much where we are, but in what direction we are moving.
–OLIVER WENDELL HOLMES

Forgiveness and Understanding

If we could read the secret history of our enemies, we should find in each man's life sorrow and suffering enough to disarm all hostility.
–HENRY WADSWORTH LONGFELLOW

It is in pardoning that we are pardoned.
–SAINT FRANCIS OF ASSISI

To err is human; to forgive, divine.
–ALEXANDER POPE

When you make a mistake, don't look back at it long. Take the reason of the thing into your mind and then look forward. Mistakes are lessons of wisdom.
The past cannot be changed. The future is yet in your power.
–HUGH WHITE, U.S. POLITICIAN (1773–1840)

If you haven't forgiven yourself something,
how can you forgive others?
–Dolores Huerta

Life as a Journey

It is good to have an end to journey toward; but it is the
journey that matters in the end.
–Ursula K. LeGuin

The really happy man is one who can enjoy the scenery on a detour.
–Anonymous

Kindness

Kindness is the language which the deaf can hear
and the blind can see.
–Mark Twain

What wisdom can you find that is greater than kindness?
–Jean-Jacques Rousseau

Be kind, for everyone you meet is fighting a hard battle.
–Philo

Give the world the best you have and the best will come back to you.
–Madeline Bridges

Hope

We judge of man's wisdom by his hope.
–RALPH WALDO EMERSON

Believe that life is worth living, and your belief
will help create that fact.
–WILLIAM JAMES

He who does not hope to win has already lost.
–JOSÉ JOAQUIN OLMEDO

If winter comes, can spring be far behind?
–PERCY BYSSHE SHELLEY

The lowest ebb is the turn of the tide.
–HENRY WADSWORTH LONGFELLOW

Resources

The following pages will give you a sampling of the enormous number of resources for help, hope, and inspiration during your teen and preteen years. Some resources can help you in a time of crisis (see the Phone Numbers at the end of this section), whereas others are great reminders of hope (see the Chicken Soup series of books listed in the Books section). It is impossible to list all the books and websites related to preteen and teen issues. More are becoming available all the time, so if the ones listed here don't fit your needs, check your bookstore, library, and the Internet for additional resources.

The resources listed in this section are organized under the following categories:

+ Books for Girls
+ Books for Boys
+ Books for Girls and Boys
+ Magazines

✦ Organizations and Websites
✦ Phone Numbers

Books for Girls

Odd Girl Out: The Hidden Culture of Aggression in Girls by Rachel
    Simmons (Harcourt, Inc. 2002)
Odd Girl Out is filled with real-life stories about the teen culture of
mean girls: bullies, cliques, attempts to ruin other girls' reputations,
and exclusion from social groups. Simmons discusses good and bad
ways of dealing with this type of aggression.

Queen Bees and Wannabes by Rosalind Wiseman (Three Rivers
    Press/Random House, 2002)
This *New York Times* bestseller, the basis for the movie *Mean Girls*
(2004, Paramount Pictures), helps both parents and girls deal with
mean and nasty teenage girls, cliques, and other teen challenges: teasing, gossiping, dating, relationships, drugs and drinking, and peer
pressure at parties.

*Mean Chicks, Cliques, and Dirty Tricks: A Real Girl's Guide to
    Getting through the Day with Smarts and Style* by Erika V. Shearin
    Karres (Adams Media Corporation, 2004)
Mean Chicks, Cliques and Dirty Tricks identifies and helps you
understand the different types of mean girls—the "snob," the "bully,"
the "teaser," the "traitor," the "clique chick," and others—what
makes them the way they are, why they act the way they do, and
what you can do about them. This well-organized book makes it
easy to find the answers you need to help you deal with these types
of girls and provides quotes from real-life teens to help bring its
message to life.

The Care and Keeping of Friends by Nadine Bernard Westcott
   (American Girl Library, 1996)
The Care and Keeping of Friends discusses how to choose and make
good friends, how to be a good friend, and how to keep friendships. It
also describes fun activities for friends to do together. This book was
written for girls, but its numerous words of wisdom about friendship
can apply to boys too.

The Girls Guide to Life by Catherine Dee (Little, Brown and Company,
   2005)
The Girls Guide to Life is both a girl's teen self-help book and an
educational book about the social issues affecting girls and women.
This interesting and highly informative book discusses issues such as
self-esteem and body image and provides strategies for dealing with
sexism, sexual harassment, and anti-girl bias in society.

Girlology: A Girl's Guide to Stuff That Matters by Melisa Holmes,
   and Trish Hutchison (Health Communications, Inc. 2005)
Written by two female doctors with daughters of their own, this book
is an excellent guide to understanding friends, relationships, boys, your
body and body image, sex and sexuality, and what the authors call
"Girl Power": the power to shape your life and be confident making
decisions and choices that matter for your life.

Being a Girl: Navigating the Ups and Downs of Teen Life by Kim Cattrall
   and Amy Briamonte (Little, Brown and Company, 2006)
Actress Kim Cattrall offers her own advice on growing up, dealing
with your parents, finding who you really are, learning self-control
and more. She blends this advice with her own teenage experiences
such as struggling with self-esteem and self-image, making mistakes,
living through her parent's divorce, and taking risks for her dreams of
being an actress. Cattrall's book is a wonderful and visually appealing book for girls.

Books for Boys

100 Things Guys Need to Know by Bill Zimmerman (Free Spirit
   Publishing, 2005)
Zimmerman offers 100 useful tips and words of wisdom for adolescent
boys such as "You're one of a kind," "Get your sleep," "Communication
is important," "School is your first career," "Do what's right for you,"
and many more.

The Guy Book: An Owner's Manual by Mavis Jukes (Random House,
   2002)
Written in a fun style of an automobile or auto mechanic's manual, this
book provides an "owner's manual" for your growing and changing
body, teenage experiences with girls and shaving, and difficult decisions about smoking, drugs, drinking alcohol, and sex. Although the
style of the book is fun, some teens might be uncomfortable with its
sometimes tell-it-like-it-is explicit language.

Books for Girls and Boys

The 7 Habits of Highly Effective Teens by Sean Covey (Fireside
   Books, 1998)
The 7 Habits of Highly Effective Teens Workbook by Sean Covey
   (Fireside Books, 2004)
These books are a teen adaptation of Steven Covey's *The 7 Habits of
Highly Effective People*. The seven habits focus on behavior modifi-
cations such as "Begin with the end in mind," or "Think win–win."
These seven strategies can help you change the way you *do* things or
think about things and as a result improve your life. Along the way to
teaching those seven strategies, Covey does a great job of providing
words of wisdom about self-esteem and self-image and making the
best choices you can make.

The 6 Most Important Decisions You'll Ever Make by Sean Covey
(Fireside Books, 2006)
As its title indicates, this book is designed to guide you through what the author considers the six most important decisions you'll make during your teen years—"make or break" decisions that can affect you for many years. This visually appealing book is loaded with colorful illustrations and quizzes that make it fun to read despite the heavy topics it sometimes addresses.

Life Strategies for Teens by Jay McGraw (Fireside Books, 2002)
Life Strategies for Teens Workbook by Jay McGraw (Fireside Books, 2001)
Daily Life Strategies for Teens by Jay McGraw (Fireside Books, 2002)
These books, written by his son, are an adaptation of Dr. Phillip C. McGraw's *Life Strategies*, which were originally written for adults. *Life Strategies for Teens* offers ten "laws" or strategies to help you take control of your teen life and where it's headed. Its "laws" such as "You cannot change what you do not acknowledge," "Life is managed, not cured," and "There is power in forgiveness," are useful not only for your teen and preteen years but also for the rest of your life.

Closing the Gap: A Strategy for Bringing Parents and Teens Together by Jay McGraw (Fireside Books, 2001)
The goal of this book is to help teens and their parents close the generational, communication, and emotional understanding gaps between them, not just to make the teenage years easier but also to help parents raise teenagers who will become confident and safe young adults. *Closing the Gap* has a great list of "do's," "don'ts," and "landmines" to help guide teens and their parents when communicating with each other.

The Complete Idiot's Guide to Surviving Peer Pressure for Teens by
Hilary Cherniss and Sara Jane Sluke (Alpha, 2002)

Surviving Peer Pressure for Teens teaches you to understand what
is and what isn't peer pressure, the types of peer pressure (how you
dress, smoking, sex, drugs, drinking, and others), how to deal with
peer pressure without losing your friends, and how to avoid your
own urge to pressure people into doing things they don't want to do.
As with the other books in the popular "Idiot's Guide" series, this
book does an excellent job of explaining issues and summarizing the
important points of each chapter or concept.

Don't Sweat the Small Stuff for Teens by Richard Carlson (Hyperion,
2000)

This book provides 100 words of wisdom for teens, many focused
on putting life into perspective, such as "Don't sweat the breakups,"
"Make peace with your mistakes," "Don't let your low moods trick
you," and "Trust your inner signals."

Growing and Changing: A Handbook for Preteens by Kathy McCoy
and Charles Wibbelsman (Perigee, 2003)

Understanding puberty, your changing body, and changing feelings
is the focus of this book. *Growing and Changing* is a highly informative and educational health-ed/sex-ed book that reads more like a
schoolbook or medical book rather than a teen self-help book (there
are no comic strips or colorful illustrations). Homeschoolers looking
for a good health-ed/sex-ed book might consider this one.

High School's Not Forever by Jane Bluestein and Eric D. Katz (Health
Communications, Inc. 2005)

High School's Not Forever is a great guide for dealing, in a positive
way, with the many potentially negative things you might experience
in high school: peer pressure; teasing about your weight, appearance,
or religion; dating and breakups; school violence; and more. Quotes
from dozens of teens add a great touch of reality to this book.

Out of the Darkness: Teens Talk about Suicide by Marion Crook
  (Arsenal Pulp Press, 2004)
Marion Crook discusses her own research on teen suicide based on
interviews with teens who attempted suicide (or considered it) to find out
why and how they coped with their situation. Her book also examines
the role of parents and schools in helping teens with this issue.

*How I Stayed Alive when My Brain Was Trying to Kill Me: One
  Person's Guide to Suicide Prevention* by Susan Rose Blauner
  (William Morrow & Company, 2002)
In this compelling and important book, Blauner describes her multiple
suicide attempts, how she finally found treatments that helped, and
her revelation that most suicidal people really don't want to die. She
offers twenty-five "tricks" that suicidal persons (not just teens) can
use to survive.

Who Moved My Cheese for Teens by Spencer Johnson (G. P. Putnam's
  Sons, 2002)
The main theme of this book is how to find your way through the
maze of life's challenges to succeed during trying times. The focus of
this book is helping young people be adaptable and resilient as they,
and their lives, continually change. *Who Moved My Cheese* is a great
book for young people facing change in their lives such as parental
divorce, moving, changing schools, and changing friends.

When Something Feels Wrong by Deanna S. Pledge (Free Spirit
  Publishing, 2002)
When Something Feels Wrong is a critical book for any young person
who has suffered physical, emotional, or sexual abuse or neglect. This
book will help you understand the abuse, why it is not your fault, what
to do if you are currently being abused, and what you can do to heal
your emotional scars.

The Thundering Years: Rituals and Sacred Wisdom for Teens by Julie
 Tallard Johnson (Bindu Books, 2001)
The Thundering Years is a spiritual approach to helping teens. It is
somewhat based on Native American spirituality but draws from
several different cultures.

Power Thoughts for Teens by Louise L. Hay (Hay House, Inc.,
 2001)
Power Thoughts for Teens is a deck of fifty "affirmation" cards to
help teens find their "inner power."

*If High School Is a Game, Here's How to Break the Rules: A Cutting-
 Edge Guide to Becoming Yourself* by Cherie Carter-Scott (Doubleday,
 2001)
This book offers ten "truths" or guidelines to help you through your
teenage years on topics such as friendships, making tough choices,
questioning authority, figuring out who you are, and learning from
your mistakes.

Teens Can Make It Happen: Nine Steps for Success by Stedman
 Graham (Fireside Books, 2000)
The nine steps to success described in Graham's book focus on knowing your own strengths and desires and how to achieve what it is you
want to achieve.

*When Nothing Matters Anymore: A Survival Guide for Depressed
 Teens* by Bev Cobain (Free Spirit Publishing, 2007)
Written by the sister of rock star Curt Cobain, this book specifically
deals with depression: its signs and symptoms, the types of depression,
sources of depression, and its treatment.

The Gifted Kid's Survival Guide: A Teen Handbook (Rev. Ed.) by Judy Galbraith, Jim DeLisle, and Pamela Espeland (Free Spirit Publishing, 1996)

Gifted young people face an array of challenges: feeling like they're odd or a freak; feeling like they don't fit in with their peers; extreme boredom at school that can lead to bad behavior; and being picked on for their good grades, intelligence, or "geekiness." This book addresses those unique challenges and provides strategies for dealing with them.

What Teens Need to Succeed: Proven, Practical Ways to Shape Your Own Future (Dream It! Do It!) by Peter L. Benson, Judy Galbraith, and Pamela Espeland (Free Spirit Publishing, 1998)

This book discusses "developmental assets," that is, things in a teen's life that help him or her to develop in a positive way (e.g., family support, self-esteem, role models).

Chicken Soup for the Preteen Soul
Chick Soup for the Teenage Soul
Taste Berries for Teens
Teen Ink: What Matters

There are many books in the *Chicken Soup, Taste Berries,* and *Teen Ink* series devoted to teens and preteens. These wonderful and popular books are collections of personal experience stories for teens written by teens. Each is a treasure full of heart-warming, hopeful, and inspirational messages. Most of the stories are short, so you can read one or two at a time whenever you need an inspirational boost. For the latest titles in the series, look at the teen section of your local bookstore or library.

Magazines

The magazine stands at your local bookstore are loaded with magazines that focus on fashion, glamour, movie stars, and dating advice, but magazines that focus on life skills, learning, and helping you become a confident, positive young adult can be more difficult to find. The magazines shown below are more likely to put aside the hype in favor of information you really need to survive and thrive through your preteen and teen years.

New Moon—The Magazine for Girls and Their Dreams

New Moon (http://www.newmoon.org/index.htm) is a positive-message magazine written and edited by girls ages eight to fourteen for girls of roughly that same age. You can find *New Moon* at larger magazine stands, or you can learn more about this magazine at http://www.newmooncatalog.com.

Boy's Life

Boy's Life is the official magazine of the Boy Scouts organization, but you don't need to be a Boy Scout to subscribe to it. *Boy's Life* topics range from outdoor adventure to history, science and ecology. To learn more or subscribe, visit http://www.boyslife.org/section/magazine/.

Discovery Girls

Discovery Girls' message of positive values and self-confidence is evident even in its articles about fashion and dating. The content for this magazine (for eight- to twelve-year-old girls) is guided by a panel of twelve girls to help ensure it is appropriate and meaningful for that age group. You can learn more about *Discovery Girls* at http://www.discoverygirls.com/.

GuidePosts' Sweet 16

This bimonthly magazine for teen and preteen girls age eleven through seventeen includes real stories and feature articles about teens. The magazine says its goal is to be a positive, inspirational magazine for girls. To learn more and see highlights of the current issue, go to http://www.sweet16mag.com/.

Guideposts for Teens

Guideposts for Teens, for both boys and girls, is the teen version of *Guideposts* magazine, a magazine about Christian religious faith featuring stories about faith and personal inspiration, many written by freelance contributors. You can find limited information about this magazine at http://www.guidepostsmag.com/ or you might find a copy at your local library or bookstore.

Breakaway

This Christian-based magazine for teen boys features articles on everything from sports to worldwide social and health issues to inspiration and faith. You can learn more at http://www.breakawaymag.com/.

Brio

Brio is the girl's equivalent of *Breakaway.* It contains articles about health and beauty, religious faith, and relationships for Christian girls. Look at http://www.briomag.com/ for more information.

Organizations and Websites

Kid's Health/Teen's Health (http://www.kidshealth.org/teen)

This website, sponsored by the Nemours Foundation, has articles for teens on everything from dealing with depression, drugs, and alcohol to food, fitness, and recipes. If you type the keyword "bullying" into the search field, you'll find some great articles about bullying and cliques.

American Foundation for Suicide Prevention (http://www.afsp.org/)

AFSP is a nonprofit organization dedicated to reducing the loss of life through suicide. Check out its website for information about suicide prevention programs, education resources, and coping with loss from suicide.

American Association of Suicidology (http://www.suicidology.org/)

The AAS is a nonprofit professional organization that promotes suicide prevention programs, and educates and supports its members who are involved in suicide prevention. Its website has information on suicide support groups and suicide prevention training.

Depressed Teens (http://www.depressedteens.com)

Depressed Teens is a website devoted to teen depression education and awareness. Check out the website for facts and information about teen depression, including a video called *Day for Night: Recognizing Teenage Depression.*

Students Against Destructive Decisions (SADD) (Originally founded as Students Against Drunk Driving) (http://www.saddonline.com/)

This is the official website of the SADD organization, whose mission is to help young people make safe and healthy decisions for their lives. See the SADD website for information about SADD chapters, starting your own chapter, the SADD speaker series, the SADD national conference, and much more.

Teen Depression Information (http://www.teen-depression.info/)

This website has information about the prevention, detection, and treatment of teen depression and suicidal behavior.

Yellow Ribbon International Suicide Prevention Program (http://www. yellowribbon.org/)

Yellow Ribbon is an international, nonprofit suicide prevention program. Its website provides suicide prevention information for students, parents, and suicide survivors. Free "Ask 4 Help" cards are available for ordering on the website.

National Institute of Mental Health (http://www.nimh.nih.gov/)

This website has a wealth of information on every kind of mental health disorder. If you are concerned that you or someone you care about has a disorder, click on this website's "Health Information" link to learn how to recognize the various disorders and find out what kind of treatments are available.

Phone Numbers

Abuse
Childhelp USA's National Child Abuse Hotline:
1-800-4ACHILD (1-800-422-4453)

Teen Help
Teen Help/Talk Hotline: 1-800-273-TALK (1-800-273-8255)

Suicide Prevention
For suicide prevention hotline phone numbers, look in the front section of your phone book (usually in the first few pages) under the heading Hotline Numbers or Important Numbers, or you can call:

The National Hopeline Network:
1-800-SUICIDE (1-800-784-2433)

You can also go to http://suicidehotlines.com/ for a list of suicide hotline phone numbers.

About the Author

In addition to being a teen and preteen survivor, Chad E. Bladow is also the parent of teen and preteen children. His parenting stories have appeared in *Welcome Home* magazine published by Family and Home Network. By sharing his own personal story in this book, he hopes to inspire and motivate young people—including his own children—to persevere, survive and look to their future with hope.

Photo by Sarah Carmody

Chad has a Masters degree in Computer Science from Washington University in St. Louis. He lives in Missouri with his wife and children.

Notes

Notes

Notes

Notes

Notes

Notes

Notes

Notes

Notes

Notes

Notes